PROGRESSIVE DESIGN DILEMMA

PROGRESSIVE DESIGN DILEMMA

Design is not a matter of taste,

it's a business!

Edition 9, 2015. Jacob Lindborg. dsgnr.io

This book is dedicated to my darling wife, my loving family, my dear friends and inspiring colleagues, who all had a hand in shaping my mind and career.

PREFACE

We must let design be all that it can be, a process built on both data and emotions, restraints and visions, knowledge and experiments. We cannot follow the easy and simple process of today, the multiple theories and methods on how to exclude what is inconvenient. We must instead be inclusive and empathic, balance the process and our aspirations and reach for tomorrow.

In this book, the 1st in the progressive design series, I'll define the principles for how design can transform you as an executive, as an entrepreneur, as a manager or as a designer. Furthermore, I'll explain how design is an enterprise transformation, not a simple change. Design is an ideology for anyone involved in the design process, seeking sustaining product opportunities or new market disruptions, using customer experience design as a customer magnet.

I'll show how you think and how your thoughts can be translated to the people around you, trusting your point of view and how we all think differently, on the subject of design. From user studies, trials and errors, failures and successes, the dilemmas and theories in this book has been defined and tested through decades.

This book will define the four principles of design,

1. Your perception and how to communicate.
2. Your challenges and how to frame them, asking the hard and difficult questions.
3. Your achievements for creating designs that resonate and are measurable, in a search for the true work, your answers.
4. Your management, the product principles and visionary culture, that will support this theory and methodology.

Through this book, I will completely redefine many established terms in this industry, for the better. I will change your perception of words like; product, design, creativity, company, achievement, challenge and language. The teachings in this book, can be applied in many different constellations and work on many levels, as each word can be interpreted to fit your circumstances and resonate with your organization.

The word *product* or *experience*, refers to all types of customer services, which can be offerings, support, marketing, retail. digital applications, fashion, food, consulting, management, processes, industrial products or components of products.

The word *company* or *organization*, refers to all types of design paradigms, which can be the entire organization, startups or a single entrepreneuring department within a larger company. It can also be consultants and freelance designers, operating on their own accord, working with companies to implement design methods.

This book is written from decades of experience with digital, industrial and conceptual designs, for the highest achieving brands in the world. Through my career, I have had many diverse roles, e.g. designing luxurious speakers and televisions for Bang & Olufsen, creating artwork and games for LEGO®, concepts and marketing for Coca-Cola®, system architecture and strategies for SONY® and server engineering and tactics for Turner®. This diversity of skills, a hybrid between the technical and artistic worlds, has often been perceived with either skepticism or disbelieve in my abilities, as how can that be possible? How can you truly master that many skills, in contrast to mastering one skill? How can you be a programmer capable of creating advanced enterprise systems, while also being an artist, creating luxurious designer products?

Balance is the way I live my life. I believe that each day will define the contrast and nuance between the negative and positive. As you explore the opposite ends of the balance spectrum, you find the rich context within, as you define the borders. This belief is embedded in every thought and is the result of my career, as I pursue to understand the grey area of all oppositions.

To every weakness, there is a strength. To every light, there is a shadow. To every dilemma, there is a solution. Nothing is gained for free, but knowledge will always succeed. These are my fundamental laws of design, as a creative balance must be kept.

The ability to be a hybrid is not about weakening your abilities, but instead strengthening your perspective and understanding. People who only speak one language, don't hear nor see the contrast, while people who speak many languages strengthening their understanding, as they start to see the denominators, reaching a higher meaning in expression and articulation. Mathematics is a class that must people avoid, as in "why do I need to learn algebra?". We need to learn about diversity in all areas of knowledge, as we then learn to see the contrast, the creative grey area of knowledge. If we don't strive to understand each other, we will never be able to work towards a common goal.

DESIGN INITIATIVES

This book will explain how design can be implemented as a business model, progressively approaching design transformation in four steps, grading your company and its design initiatives. In order to define the theory, we must first understand the problem at each step.

1. **Production**, an organization who has no design implementation at all, creating products that resembles tools, packed with features to solve every conceivable use-case. This common step among production houses only deals with the challenges, the critical and data driven approach to features.

They do this because customers talk about and compare products by features, they don't talk about their feelings and how a product adds emotional value to their life. Because of this dilemma, features are often perceived as market demands, though the deeper understanding of customers demands is in the emotional value, which is the actual business driver for product loyalty.

2. **Style**, creating products with a gap between the features and the users expectations. This common step among design agencies only deals with the achievements, creating surface designs, that fools the user to bond with the surface, only to discover the hollow center, the incomplete relation to function and story, as most design agencies don't understand the technical side of product design. This step is the opposite of the first step, creating products that resonate with customers emotions, without delivering features that can match the expectations.

3. **Management**, building through phases, creating substance and validation with UX teams and clients. This common step only deals with the management and customers, engineered to fix the previous problems, without solving the issue, the creative balance, synergies, processes, perceptions and culture. These companies implement a design process for category management, where each category is solution-based, instead of story-based. If the category is based on results, you keep working from the customers end point, instead of turning it around, working from the customers

starting point, creating categories based on customers desire to solve a situation.

4. **Ideology**, where design is implemented on an executive level, delivering strategic experiences. Measuring your investments and producing resonating products. This step deals with design as it was meant to be, an enlightening business model. Improving your growth, processes, customer loyalty and organizational culture. Evolving employee knowledge and customer belief. Strengthening it all together, in a healthy balanced methodology. It implements multiple processes and principles, covering and balancing all angles of design.

Many known and popular design processes are trying to fix the problem from different angles, like lean manufacturing, CX/UX/UI principles, agile sprints and innovative solutions. But the problem is greater than one process, it's greater than one perception and must be dealt with at its core, understanding each other and the customers, through superior collaboration, knowledge and methods.

Chris Bangle, chief designer at BMW, told me about their devoted design process and how they implemented design as an ideology. Every person working in the factory must know and trust that they are designing beautiful and luxurious cars, regardless of their job title.

As a result of their implemented ideology, the factory production line is running through the entire building, from marketing to accounting. Anyone, anywhere, are constantly seeing the results of their work direct or indirect, feeling responsible for the products, as new cars are running by their office all day long.

From the cleaning staff, the cafeteria, the marketing and executives, to the guy on the factory floor, they were all part of the same organism, breathing the same belief and their shared ideology.

As one out of five projects fail so badly, on a global average, that they threaten the very existence of the company, it has become a standard practice to eliminated all elements of chance, design believed to be one of them.

Investments in design is regarded as pure cost factors, frustrating not only to designers, but also for the departments who know that design is important and adds value to their market shares and their customer base. These frightened companies are gathering their courage to take another step on the design ladder, but are held back by the lack of measurability in the chances and risks, offered by design. As we cannot measure, we cannot convince our shareholders or board of directors to invest in design. They often focus on the fragile mass market shares. Because of this dilemma, design must be more than just an addition to the product, it must be measurable and believable.

Design has become an element of production, a one sided perspective, instead the production itself. It's the little extra the customer can hope to get, when they purchase a product, which can be physical, digital or a delivered as service. Design went from the undoubtable legacy of our history, to a position of nice-to-have, a component, a checkbox on your statement of work, an option. Design is fighting for a right to exists, in a world where lean manufacturing and normalized production is competing in the great battle of consumer goods and services, discarding anything unmeasurable.

Customers don't trust ideas based on hollow visuals and shallow experiences. They believe in the story, the true concept, the core and the essence. Everything else is circumstantial, everything else is achievable, everything else is reproducible. They believe in products, where every detail is telling the same strong resonating story. They trust products that offers true feelings created by true people. They trust their emotions, thus must your product offer values that will respond to their empathy. As emotions are stronger than knowledge and logic, thus will emotional products sustain and surpass the competition.

Design as a noun, is the manifestation of objects, managing a designers perception. Design as a verb, is achieving creativity through challenges.

We all understand the word, but very few understands the implications of design, design as a business, as it has become a complex organism of individual opinions and fractured skills, spanning multiple departments, multiple people with multiple beliefs. Hence its clouded understanding and perceived intangible implementation, design has sadly fallen into a matter of taste, a degrading category of subjectivity. But as you will discover through this book, design is not a matter of taste, it's a business.

DILEMMA

Creativity is a word often perceived as a synonym for artistry, the ability to create ideas by applying methods to a process. It is also a word which often divides departments and people into the creative and the non-creative types.

In my past jobs and projects, there has always been an unfortunate negative culture, supporting the creative versus the technical minds, fighting over budgets, diversities and opinions. The creative departments feels lost in their inability to convince the technical department to support their rapid ideas and attention to details in every inch of the product. The technical department feel overburden by the unstructured and abstract nature of the creative department, unable to facilitate and bring their many perspectives to market. Furthermore, the artistic mind is often driven by visual ideas, in contrast to the technical mind, driven by results. This diversity creates priority issues on matters of opinions, that must be managed.

Every time I planted my feet on creative territory as an architect, I got the look, "Oh no, what now!". The frighten and annoyed looks from colleagues, who didn't want me to limit their ideas and change their visions into reality. They where focusing on achieving the next great thing in customer experiences.

Every time I planted my feet on technical territory as an artist, I got the look, "Oh no, what now!". The frighten and annoyed look from colleagues, who where under pressure from management and approaching deadlines, keeping their eyes on errors, which only yield a number, a narrow goal to minimize. They where focusing on challenging the limitations and finding the viable tactics.

These looks, was always the initial reaction from people who didn't know me or my progressive approach to design, as a creative hybrid between different people and different jobs.

The analytical poet is a creative story teller, envisioning the customers insight into product ideas. The engineer is a creative innovator, bringing new ideas to life through technical achievements. The architect is a creative organizer, structuring innovations into system- and user interactions. The artist is a creative expressionist, relating to the customers emotions and their ongoing experience. The project manager is a creative game keeper, keeping the ball at play, planning resources and processes. The director is a creative strategist, analyzing the market and upcoming obstacles.

Though we all have a different perspective on creativity, it is part of all job descriptions, as it is the life blood in every task performed. From algorithms and mathematical breakthroughs, to emotional and artistic experiences, we are all creative people. The ability to be creative, is the ability to be smart, intuitive and job efficient.

THE LOOSING BATTLE

When we experience fine dining, we often talk about the sweet, the sour, the hot and the cold. We talk about the things we can define and relate to. We don't talk about the combined result of all the ingredients, as we often don't know how to define it, other then rubbing our belly, expressing our delight. This result, the superb dining experience, is the combination of many ingredients and a rigorous process of perfection by the chef. When we describe a perfect bottle of wine, we again use tangible terms of sweetness or earthiness. We don't describe the essence of the wine, the sensory experience of subtle flavors, as the experience is to complex to describe. We are not capable of describing the story behind the experience, though when told, it resonates with our tastebuds.

If you focus on evolving your customer experiences, your products are merely ingredients of an experience and your churn rate is subject to the insight you seek. If you redefine your products as ingredients of an experience, then you redefine your product categorizations and customer relation, based on customer insight.

Any competitor can readily match your offer, making product differentiation a losing strategic battle. Any startup can quickly mimic your processes and methods, producing the same results as you. If your competitive advantage is design, then your competitive advantage is an ideology to deliver the best customer experiences.

Through strategic rigor, your customer experiences will create a unique proposition, as you constantly learn and evolve with your market share. This process of action and reaction, will keep you ahead of the competition, as the relation with your customers and your insight learned, isn't duplicable.

When defining the value of an experience, we often fail to define a tangible measurement, as we don't know how to measure emotions. We do know how to measure churn and satisfaction, as your executive management is following the numbers. The problem is how we define product sale, as we usually look at product numbers. But products are just an element of the overall experience, as customers don't buy products, they buy experiences. If you ask your customers, how many would buy an experience, the answers would be vague, as we often express ourselves in tangible terms, unable to tell the story. We might buy a car, but we only need the car as a proxy to achieve freedom. That same achievement might be possible by other means and if you understand your customers *means to an end,* then you know that your business shouldn't focus on the *means*, but instead the *end*.

Every tangible product sold, is in a direct relation to an intangible experience. By that definition, experiences are calculable investments and can be measured by their ingredients. If customers complain about one ingredient, your experience can simply adapt to the changes, evolving with demand. Products are not business pillars or silos of management efforts. They are merely ingredients, used in many experience offers. It's time to redefine what a product is and let your real offers come forth. The next revolutionizing product, is an experience.

DESIGNING IS A HOLISTIC EXPERIENCE

Design is when story, function and journey spins together in a spiral synergy, managed by a design team who breath and exhale its essence, driven through a design methodology by high achievers, skillful passionates and devoted aficionados.

The costumers expectations and experiences are an achievement, not a purchase, peeling the onion in a conceptual environment. Each layer will enforce the design, establishing a tethered bond and relationship with the user, tightening the believe in the product, the company, the brand.

It's not in the merits of what you see in the end result, it's about the strategy, tactics and creation in the design process. If you like what you see, then you fall into the criteria for the design, otherwise you don't. Transcend your design and emerge your organization within the core of design, creating rich customer experiences.

A phrase I often hear in my line of work, is that; design is a matter of taste. Progressive design theory states, that great design is not a matter of taste and further more, it is not created by a committee.

Design isn't just the cover of a book, the layout of a website, the poster of a movie or the exterior of a car. Design is everything, from thoughts to execution, from story to experience, from strategy to creation, from expectations to feelings, from possessions to recommendations, from statistics to marketing, from packaging to in-store purchase.

Design is the book that ignites my expectations, infused by the touch of the cover. It's the weight against my lab, as I sit down with a great roast of coffee. It's the first smell of the paper, the memories that flows through my mind of previous experiences holding such a book. It's caressing the first page, letting my eyes browse through the words. It's each chapter indulging my adventurous mind, delivering the story with enticing precision. It's the final page, the gratification and the fulfillment. It's my recommendations, my devoted believe in this book experience and that my friends will love this experience too.

Design is the adverb resonating in my head, as I type my search into Google, locating the first result, rendering the first fold. It's is the colors and typography of the website, dividing my attention, adding focus and direction. It's the ingenious interaction, intuitively unfolding as I approach each layer of information. It's the playful delivery of entertainment and communication as I browse the online experience. It's the sense of security and comfort as I add to my shopping basket. It's the statistics processed in the background, as I enjoy the moment, getting tailored suggestions in personalized surroundings. It's the following email, confirming my purchase, insuring my comfort and further interest in the product catalogue, gaining my trust.

Design is the first sight of a movie poster at my neighborhood bus-stand, getting excited about the actors and the story told in simple images and clever phrases. It's calling my friends, arranging tickets, reserving the local burger joint. It's the sound of the cinema hall and the aroma of popcorns. It's the walk towards our seats, getting comfortable and guessing the intermediate quiz show. It's the commercials and trailers. It's the orchestrated sound and video of the movie, as the minutes fly by, letting me submerge my mind and body within the theater. It's delivering a journey of exceeded expectations, demanding more, followed by "to be continued".

Design is the sight of a truly luxurious car, as the sun hits its curves and the colors bounce against the reflexions. It's the sound of the door closing as I leans back, embraced by the leather, surrounded by serene silence. It's the anticipation of the engine, as I jingle the keys, adventuring over the dashboard. It's the emotional thrust, as the engine explodes, forcing the silence into submission, from the roar of the cylinders. It's the beautiful digital display of the dashboard and the intuitive GPS guidance anticipating my moves and needs, with a soothing, comfortable and choreographed voice, creating an emotional bond with the car. It's when I reach my destination and the ride is coming to an unwanted stop.

Design is a business, and as such, you must be able to define and understand its entirety, thereby measure and trust all aspects of the process, validating your investments. Creating a product based on progressive design, will ensure a resonating and perfect adapted solution for your target group. Embedding design in your organization will bring perspective to your investments, infusing your products with substance, quality and loyalty.

THE PRINCIPLE THEORY

Great theories are build on dynamic circumstances, i.e. being built for an adaptive solution. In order to process the design dilemma, we must first define the principles and terms, to categorize design.

The dilemma of progressive design, defines four principles, each detailed in subsequent principles. The four principles brings a different contrast and mindset to the process and will help you uncover hidden perspectives in your design, balancing all angles, as you build from the inside out, keeping the customer at the center.

There are many processes and theories influencing design, most prominent is lean and measurable processes, engineered to create designs based on data and specifications. From both development houses and design agencies, different perspectives and angles are shaping the solutions, as they manage the process based on their offerings. But the truth is, that they are all right and wrong at the same time, as the answer is in the grey area.

Design is not just a question about data, process or approach, as the initial principles must be based on the goal, to design a creative balanced product, through and through. From the people and teams involved in the product, to the management ruling the process and shaping the culture. From the critical limitations and concerns, to the disruptive blue sky opportunities and budget shortcuts.

The four primary principles of design are,

1. **Perceive**, communicating your story, infusing the message, delivering the vision. Design must be emotional, for it to be believable. As a designer, you must understand your customers, yourself, your capabilities and how to express them.
2. **Challenge**, the discovery of questions, broadening your horizon and defining your canvas with critical questions. Design limitations must be known, as wide or narrow they might be. Knowledge is the key to challenge your designs.
3. **Achieve**, searching for the hidden meaning, connecting the dots, answering your questions, declaring your creativity in iterations. Design must evolve, as a story, derived from rapid prototyping.

4. **Manage**, a visionary culture, carving your rosetta stone, to lead your product rules and principles through lean and agile development, defining your inputs and outputs. Design must be cultivated, based on a shared ideology. Establishing a design language and a strong team, is vital for the design manager.

As there must be a balance in design, so do the four principles balance each other. Perception is balancing management and challenges are balancing achievements.

The tangible work are your challenges and achievements, also described as the why and how. A double question that you must remember as an initial thought to every decision you make.

The intangible work is your perception and management, also described as your abstract mind and your directional culture.

The tangible and intangible creates two axis of design, where each pole is balancing you path, to create a meaningful magical moment with the customer at the center.

CHAPTER 1

PERCEIVE

"Design is a mindset, a passion,
from which your vision will be told."

Through these pages, you will learn, that you are not alone in your struggles and that your mind can achieve a higher understanding by being stronger through your own thoughts.

In this chapter, I will depict four fictional people, representing a way of thinking, dividing your thoughts and actions into relatable faces. Some people favor one more then the others, while the hybrid designer master all four. The importance is to understand your divided mind and learn to improve each side, as we are all hybrids.

The old Egyptian fables tells the story about a poet who wanted to tell an abstract story about the afterlife, conceptualizing and celebrating death and culture. An engineer used the brick to build the foundation, creating a strong platform for the entire vision. An architect sees the bigger picture, a triangular shape that explores the foundation into new heights. An artist wrote the story in hieroglyphs, incorporating the architecture, aligning the stars, covering the walls in iconic tales, that still stands today.

The principles of design perception are,

1. **Poet**, the visionary. Design must be poetic, meaningful and solve insightful user needs, be relatable and believable.
2. **Engineer**, the innovator. Design must be engineered and magical, with practical poised innovation. Users don't buy purpose-based products, they buy situation-based products.
3. **Architect**, the mentalist. Design must be understood, as it must understand the user, build on intuitive architecture.
4. **Artist**, the communicator. Design must be emotional, i.e. humorous, delightful or serious, identifying with the users lifestyle through artistic expressions.

Design is a perception, an approach to communicating a vision, told by the mind of the insightful poet, the innovative engineer, the structured architect and the emotional artist, working together, forming the perfect designed product, each from a different perspective.

Perception is in the eye of the beholder, a mindset, from which communication will be an illusion. 'Theory of the Mind' is a psychology term for defining our ability to be self aware and perceive the mind of other people. Your design ideas are pieces, painted on a canvas in your mind. This painting is unknown to me and my perception will make it blurry. I won't understand, what you can't explain.

Translating this vision into a tangible design, is a perceptive language of signs, codes and their intertwine meaning. To communicate without interference, we must be able to understand our shared perspective, as you must be able to see my point of view.

The four characters manifest a collective mind, the eye of providence to challenges and achievements, working with design as a unified mind, reaching the user with a coherent product, a resonating story.

The mind is capable of subtle, curved, linear and abstract thoughts, embodying the spirit of the entire product, not just visualizing and prototyping ideas, but creating poetry and simplicity through a journey of user expectations, told in a design language.

Switching from one perception to another, based on the task at hand, is eminent to implementing ideas, inspiration and guidelines from the people around you. Having the capacity to be visionary, technical and creative in equal measures, a hybrid, gives you a unique ability to conceptualize and create what others can't, see the bigger picture, connecting the dots.

EVERYTHING IS RELATIVE

Here is a hard fact, you will never fully understand this book and you will never fully understand my teachings. It has nothing todo with your ability to learn or comprehend, but is based on a human conundrum; my cognitive experience is uniquely mine. You might get the essence of my intended teachings, carefully put into words, but my mind will never be transcended into these pages. Therefore, you can only get a glimpse of my perspective and hopefully, you will piece it together in the same order as I.

Every word, every sentence, every color, every image, has a different meaning to me as it has to you. There are many common misconceptions about predefined values for these elements of design. Each cognitive input will emerge as an illusive image in your mind, from which you build your perception. That image is a unique imprint, that no amount of words or illustrations will be able to duplicate, it's yours, and yours alone and you can only hope to let me understand a fraction of your perception.

You might have noticed that I frequently repeat synonyms of the same word and explain the same sentence from different angels. I do this to replicate my perception to you, my reader, narrating across these words of mine, trying to understand my teachings and intensions in each phrase. Depending on how well my explanations are, these sentences will make your reading feel familiar and comfortable, as we approach a common ground of understanding.

Color definitions suggest that each color has a specific meaning, e.g. that green is a calm color and that pink is a feminine color. These suggestions are subjective, and as a designer, you must work from a perspective that everything is relative. Anything can be branded and anything branded can change.

Many centuries ago, the color pink was the brightest color a man could wear and was therefore considered the strongest color to show your power and virility among men. Men wore the pink color with all the pride one could bestow.

Women was considered weak and wore therefore cheap dark blue colors. These where not the colors of strong powerful men, and the blue color was branded with shame.

It's fair to say, that these colors have a completely different brand and perception today. The dark blue color is a color of power, worn by people in authority, while the pink color is branded with feminine virtues.

A DESIGNERS HEARTACHE

Most designers fall in love, literally, with their work and are incapable of adapting, unable to convey their perception. This can be a beautiful love story if they are meant for each other or it can be a world of heartache if they are on two different tracks.

I know I love you, I know you love me, but this can't go on. We are not right for each other, we don't belong together. You're mine and I'm yours, but we must both find new relations apart. I'm trying to bend you into something that you're not meant to be. I'm trying to hold on for as long as I can, only ending up destroying your nature, your purity, your spirit.

You are a child of my mind, my thoughts and dreams, your are a fabric of my creativity, my poetic expression. This bond between us will be hard to break, but I must do it, for I'm blinded by my devotion to you, my fascination by the things that we could have been, but never will!

As a designer, an artist, a concept developer, you'll know of this heartache, this pain in your chest when you must aside from your design, your concept, your idea and turn towards new horizons.

Heartache happens when you realize that you are misguided by your own thoughts, trapped, because of your devotion and creative exploration of your concept, leading you into compromising ideas. The story, the idea, the concept is so captivating, that it has blinded your judgement, hunted by an abstract expression.

Heartache happens when your team hits you with the reality, the truth and possibilities of your resources, limiting the technical foundation that your idea was born upon, creating disbelieve and frustration towards the people who where only trying to support your ideas from their perspective.

Heartache happens when your client isn't buying your idea, creating relationship tension, anger and abandonment. You don't won't to understand the client and the client can't understand what you can't explain. Your perceptions are not aligned and you need to restart with the fundamentals, sharing insights and declaring expectations, understand each other.

Be true to your self, be true to your ideas. Don't comprise, don't let your ideas rule your product goals, let the product goals inspire your ideas. If your ideas are being compromised, let it go, start over, rethink. Truly great ideas are born strong and can't be compromised, they will ensure signature experiences that will deliver iconic products and will inspire new solutions in their path. Don't be afraid to let go of an idea that won't resonate with your team, client or customers.

It just wasn't meant to be.

DESIGN ADOPTION IS A BITTER PILL TO SWALLOW

Adopting another designers work is never easy, it goes against the nature of a designer, being a creator, a frontier. Design is a believe, rooted deeply within, a culture in some cases. We don't feel for what we can't see, we don't understand what we can't comprehend, we need context, an angle, a common ground. We need the same perception.

When adopting a design, you must embrace its presence, understand the language and let it become a fluent dialogue from your tongue. You must know that your pride and creativity is not degraded by this new adopted believe, but instead, it will challenge your thoughts and broaden your horizon, strengthen your skills. You must be accepting and rely on your knowledge, your success and self-confidence, be stronger and better than just one ideology.

You must emerge from your zone and see that each adopted design is a book, one you must read and fully understand, before you can judge the cover. When you have read and understood the book, then you can make it yours, take responsibility, ownership and improve. Let the design evolve with your thoughts, but respect its legacy, the thoughts that came before yours.

The ability to embrace the work of others, is your empathy, your creative mind at its best. When you stop labeling, stop assuming and dive into your curiosity, your empathy will unlock hidden levels of creativity, strengthen your skills and expand your mind. Empathy is derived from a strong creative soul and nourished through shared teachings. Unlock your mind, your empathy, your creativity and your assumptions.

BATTLE OF INSECURITY

When working in teams, collaborating over solutions and strategies, opinions and principles fly in all directions. We all have something that we would like to share and contribute to the project, an investment in logic and feelings. When the storm settles, the insecurity starts to emerge between the different personalities.

We all wanted to be heard and we all wanted to be a vital part of the process. We need to believe in our opinions because we need to exists, our opinions must matter. When we are challenged and our opinions starts to crumble from lack of strength, our will to survive takes over. It's a survival instinct and our brain can't process consequences as it needs to react quickly, fight or flight. It replaces logic with the invested feelings, instincts, manifested in opinions that are driven into a defensive direction, where you can withstand a feasible fight.

Your opinions have been heard and discussed, but haven't made any difference. They have been validated and was discarded.

They have been turned and inspected from all angles, without acknowledgment. You feel empty, as your investment falls apart, your time and effort gone to waste. Anger and defiance emerges as you must have the final word, your opinion can't die, it must be a valid opinion, as you must be validated.

"Why don't they understand me?"

"Why can't they see the importance as I do?"

You start fighting for your discredited opinion, as you know this is your last stand, backed against the wall, instead of finding a new and stronger position. The product becomes a hostage in this battle of insecurity, as you start to drill into the bedrock foundation that everyone is building upon, the story, the strategy, the insight. You try to bend and shape all knowledge into a scenario that will support your opinion. Your survival instinct is taking you and the project into the wrong direction and you must overcome this basic human behavior to turn it around. You must know when to battle your primal nature and when to let go of your ideas.

You must be stronger than your personal needs and put aside your aspirations and ego, giving in to the team, learn from your peers and become better, stronger and wiser. Design is about inspiration and seeking the bigger picture, broadening your perception, not fighting for an ideology that only applies to your needs.

SHAPING YOUR PERCEPTION

Ideology is a cultivated set of ideas, a psychological concept orbiting principles, methods and emotions, in your universe of thoughts. We use ideologies to guide and define a sense of belonging, a sense of self control, a sense of comfort. Following a diet, religious believes or using a code of honor, is a personal ideology, shaping your mind, your perception. Rooted deeply within, we fight for our point of view, as we fight for our ideology from which we form our perception of what is right and wrong. This fight can be an extremely emotional battle, as our ideology can be a strong and tethered bond, tightly wrapped around our entire self believe, our successes and relations.

As the bond grows stronger, the ability to break it will subside, only succeeded by a competing ideology, attracting your perception into a new orbit. Battles, discussions or conflicts, formed over ideologies, is a collision course, fighting for the idea that you believe is right, so deeply.

We use ideology to calm a stressful situation, improve our faith, solving problems and guide us through difficult decisions, creating a mental path of success. But there is no such thing as luck, being successful or having a hot streak. Statistically, we will all have success, and as humans we emphasize such coincidences, forgetting the math, the logic. We use these occurrences and patterns to form meaningful impressions, leading them into our ideology as proof. If you emphasize on the negative, you form a disbelieve in yourself and your abilities, as these memories will build up, forming a negative perception. You'll see yourself or your project as a failure.

Believing in math and logic, as a design ideology, will state that there is no such thing as failures and success, only how we emphasize these occurrences. You are as successful as you perceive yourself to be, as it's all in your mind.

Through my personal life and career, I've always had a strong believe in my self and my abilities. Not because of my knowledge or my perception of success, but because of a simple statistical fact that I learned as early as the 6th grade from my math teacher, "sooner or later, it will happen". With passion, patience and confidence, you'll achieve success, but the same ideology will also prepare you for the unavoidable failures.

You'll decide what you'll remember from the meaningful occurrences in your life, good or bad, what you'll learn and how you choose to build your self believe. Defining your self is not a job title, but a believe, a personal brand, build on the ideologies that orbit your mind. Thinking like a poet, engineer, architect and artist, your mind is capable of achieving all obstacles, as you have the potential to balance your thoughts from all four angles.

WHEN YOUR SKILLS BECOME PASSÉ

The worst fate you can give your skills, is to let them become your identity, your pride and your job title. Skills will eventually become outdated, passé, and your goal is to always be ahead, analyzing the knowledge pool, building one skill-set upon another, crawling the experience latter.

Wordpress, a revolutionizing CMS system, has been part of my toolbox for many years, way beyond the early nostalgic years when Wordpress was 'just' a blogging framework. Through the latest years, I have personally used and misused the system to perform the unimaginable. I have fully enjoyed the concept and the many projects that have been build upon this beautiful architecture, delivered by the Wordpress core team. Projects like traditional websites, advanced HTML5 games, API web-services and comprehensive enterprise systems have all come to life from this toolbox of mine.

Wordpress has been able to submit to all my needs as an engineer, an architect and a designer. But Wordpress is no ordinary CMS system anymore and is now the system of choice for most developers, used for private and enterprise solutions. It is the backbone of most websites and with a wast growing pool of advanced themes and plugins, the system is almost unstoppable.

This growth is driven by independent developers and web agencies, who build their name and success on this platform, a platform that might soon be passé?

The problem with Wordpress is the fundamental truth and brilliance from the Wordpress team, it is just too easy to use. As an engineer, the architecture is simple to get started with and within minutes, your project is coming to life. As a designer, the interface is intuitive and creative, a smart and engaging CMS system for all users; the developer, the administrator and the visitor.

This interface can be populated with an almost unlimited amount of themes and plugins, shaping your solution with simple clicks, no technical skills needed. Automated hosting services are offering on-click solutions, with a preconfigured Wordpress installation, just use 5 minutes and your website is ready to go public.

These trends are shaping the internet everywhere, creating cloud-based applications and systems that will manage your life and needs with ease. The idea of a web agency is quickly becoming a thing of the past, making advanced technology available to the general public, invalidating years of learning and expertise in the process. The internet is normalizing our problems and frustrations through highly specialized and targeted services, offering all the tools you need to create iconic websites with perfect SEO integration, high-performance hosting service and responsive design technics, all achieved in minutes and just under a few dollars.

In this intuitively managed and fully serviced internet utopia, where is the need for a skilled developer or even a full service web agency?

We need to move on and beyond our skills. Wordpress is now part of the trending internet culture and is quickly becoming a developers past skill-set, loosing traction to the automated systems and joining past technologies like Perl and Adobe Flash® for web. Wordpress is not becoming outdated or deprecated, just mainstream, a developers nostalgic moment in time, while we continue to fuel our brains with new disruptive technologies and work on the next revolutionizing system that will outdate Wordpress eventually.

SECTION 1

POET

As a design poet, you are a dreamer, living in the moment, feeling the world around you and the implications it has, as it turns. You can think in subtle thoughts, finding the true essential meaning in everything, interlinked by a mesmerizing story, a deeper meaning, revealing the poetry of your products existence.

You are a concept author, a story teller, writing the very fabric of your product, the DNA, which will be part of an evolutionary timeline, maturing your products and testing your poetic vision.

You are the abstract mind, working on multiple levels, in multiple dimensions. As a poet, you wonder, you explore, you question every facet in your cognitive experience, as a warm summer breech. You are opinionated, as you seek to understand everything and believe in every understanding. You enjoy these thoughts, they soots you and the world seems to make sense, as your unravel a hidden meaning. Your understand the secrets and live to discover their purpose.

You are a visionary and accelerates in ideas, concepts and the resulting products. You are the inspiration and trendsetter of the team, an evolutionary force, moving and engaging your audience and the products they use.

The overly passionated and eccentric designers are more abstract in their deliveries and abstraction lowers a customers expectations, creating an accepting state of mind, towards what must be the work of a beautiful mind, accepting the transience of imperfection.

Fueling your designs with an element of abstraction, can help build mystery and magic in your creations. Adventure beyond the safe lines, towards a great story telling. A little eccentricity can go a long way, giving your product an edge and a poetic soul.

I was wondering, thoughts where drifting, searching for a place to rest. I was looking for an epiphany, I was looking for a picture, the bigger picture. There must be something there, there must be a hidden meaning, something I haven't thought of or haven't discovered.

Suddenly a puzzle piece was offered to me in a quick conversation with an old friend of mine. This new information, this fact was going through my mind as a pattern without a home. I needed to sit down.

I searched the far edges of my mind, looking for a place to lay my thoughts to rest, as my face suddenly froze, immobile by the rush of thoughts. Pieces fighting in an emerging epiphany, a sudden silence before the storm. The thunder, the rush, the adrenalin exploded and revealed a clarity, brightening my senses, blowing my mind.

I jumped up from my beloved chair, with a smile dividing my face, my blood wash rushing through my vanes and every thought I had was going in one direction; I had just discovered a revolution.

I needed a pen, I needed to get my reflections into something tangible. I wanted to take a print of my mind and share it with the world. The feelings was overwhelming as I scribbled my conclusions into my laptop, commemorating the picture into words. I had a moment, it was so vivid, flushing over my entire body, as I rigorously pored my heart into each sentences.

I'm a poet.

SECTION 2

ENGINEER

As a design engineer, your primary drive is functionality, creating the core of the product. You don't care about how parts are fitting together or how they look. You only care about what parts you could invent and enrich the possibilities of the product with. You are an idea machine, an inventor, an innovator.

You are the linear mind, calculating the algorithm and processing chunks of information into ideas, the innovator of the team. You would be aware of all the tools in the universe and solving problems is only a question about finding the right tool for the right job. If possible, you would create new tools for solving new problems, puzzle pieces, laying the foundation for your team, the bedrock.

Your estimates are sometimes delayed by a continues stream of great ideas. This could result in over-engineering or refactoring repeatedly, beyond the deadline. The product can either suffer or succeed from this behavior, as there is often a thin line between great work and late work.

You keep asking the same question; how could I improve the mechanics of my design, the very essence of the product you are creating. You have a mindset that despise regularities and celebrate every nuance in the world around you. You are the true definition of a nerd and will dive into every detail in your path, to understand it and break it, to rebuild a better and a stronger version.

You don't see your technical insight as a limitation toward creating the next generation in design, clouded by what you know to be possible, you see your knowledge as a stepping stone towards greater heights. You know what is possible, you know what could be possible and you now what will become possible.

You are a developer with the capacity to dive into another world, far away from this place and time. In this world you find solutions to the most complex problems, as you zoom in on the minute details, stopping time in the process, observing.

When you are in the zone, everything around you, is cut off. Your brain is working at triple speed and all senses are focusing on the problem ahead. You don't see or hear the people around you. You don't even notice the time. You are not available, you are in the zone.

You are always looking for the next fix, the adrenalin rush, the next problem to solve, and you do that by loosening knots. You are a nerd in the best possible way, solution attentive beyond measures. When the knot is conquered, you feel an overwhelming satisfaction by the achievement and the dopamine rush pushes you to the next knot, to the next fix, to the next high.

The ultimate fix, is when you find a solution to all the knots at once, the one solution to rule them all. In this state, you become god of your world. This is the adrenalin rush that will spark innovation and dedication to the product. This is the state of mind that you are searching for, and with out it, you become bored of the situation, the product and your job. Keeping you in a constant search for problems and ensuring victories, is the catalyst to innovative functionality that will enrich the product and the company.

At a monday morning product meeting, my colleague, a project manager, asked the simple and friendly question, "how was your weekend?".

In my engineering mind, the question was outside the scope of the meeting, getting the product process organized. The question only created another problem to solve, so I answered the question in a quick and concise manner, "it was fine, thanks!", and followed the answer with a smile.

A minute pasted by and my colleague started to get an expression on his face that mimed the sentence, "don't you want to know about my weekend?", in an awkward silence. I was compelled to reverse the question, and "How was Your weekend?", i asked.

It's not that I didn't care about his weekend, I just didn't se it as relevant when I was focusing on problems at hand, getting the optimal out of any situation, seeing small-talk as inefficient dialog, in this context.

I'm an engineer.

SECTION 3

ARCHITECT

As a design architect, you demand control, taxonomy and structure in every aspect of your product, orchestrating the customer journey. You are the king of logic and everything needs to fit together and become standardized. You are driven by intuitive controls and recursive structures, to satisfy your lust for streamlining the functionality and behaviors of your product. You have a mindset that will eliminate every irregularities and polish every scratch in your work, to create a useable and understandable product.

You have a curved mind, bending the engineers thoughts and results, shaping their great ideas into structured solutions, zooming out, speeding up time. You don't like when things are out of place, when your line of sight is disturbed in any way. You are the order, the ruler of rules.

You are the structured member of the team. Like the engineer, you are aware of all the tools in the universe, but solving problems is a question about finding the perfect tool for the perfect job. You see the bigger picture, taking the puzzle pieces and connecting the dots, as the image emerge, discovering the solutions.

As an architect, you are responsible for classifying problems and opportunities, to order and structure the process into a solid foundation, feasible of getting traction from all departments. The most common problem in product development, is the lack of a well founded architecture to highlight and communicate the product capabilities. Architecture must understand and streamline customer, system and product interactions, as an adaptable platform, supporting future changes.

I was visiting my favorite Italian restaurant with my family, and ten minutes into the evening, i suddenly realized that I had rearranged the two tables that we where sitting at, lining them up perfectly next to each other. I had even put a small piece of napkin under one leg, to raise the table, to form a smooth surface between the two of them, giving the illusion that we where sitting at one long table. The forks, knifes and plates where all in a perfect alignment and I began to organize the glass in a perfect angle between the plate in front of me and the table borders.

This is when I realized the unspoken attention I got from my family, who all had a smile on there faces uttering the words, "What are you doing?".

I was simply creating order and minimizing redundancy in my path.

I'm an architect.

DISCOVERING TAXONOMY

As an architect, you look for optimizations, how to group and categorize every element of the design process. This can be anything from visuals and business strategies, to the technical architecture and productional process.

While you search for the optimal solution, remember to be aware of the real customer-centric classifications, as you can end up trying to solve what isn't ready or right to be solved, from a customers circumstantial perspective.

If we look at the markets where most people are investing time and money in finding solutions, we start to see where there is an issue and a demand to find the ultimate solution, the architectural solution. Though these indicators might guide you into your next project or business venture, trying to categorize the problem and defining a theory, you must remember that sometime you can't simplify the problem as a taxonomy structure, as the problem might not be one problem at all.

In project management, there are thousands of software offers, which are all sold under the title, "One solution to all your needs!". A tempting headline, as the need to solve a project managers schedule, is always of the essence. Though there are many offers, all trying to solve the problem, even stating that fact, they are neglecting the initial story, that a project managers schedule is as unique to me, as it is to you. There is no singular solution to a project managers schedule, as each project manager is working as a customized installment in the company. There are best practices, but even the best practice is changing between different industries and organizations. If you want to solve the project managers daily rituals, you must be aware of their circumstances.

In any industry, in any organizational structure, there are many problems to be solved by the architectural mind. Most of them can be solved by finding the right classifications, building a theory on insightful taxonomy.

As an architect, you know of this work, as it's your fundamental practice in all your decisions. Though it might be a fundamental way of working, it is one of the hardest thing to get right, classifying issues into a structured solution. You must be able to describe the problem, classify the issues and theorize your solution. The ability to choose the right classifications, is the ability to see the problem, analyzing the circumstance.

Many startup companies and their solutions has been brought to life, building on a blind assumption that they can fix the problem, but fails to do so. They haven't found the right way to structure the problem and the process, unable to create a true customer-centric product and theorize a great architectural taxonomy. If you can create the ultimate theory to a product, you can change the market completely, shifting into a new gear. The ability to create this taxonomy, is the secret to an architects success.

SECTION 4

ARTIST

As an artist, painter, illustrator and communicator of feelings and values, you understand a wide array of emotions and are able to communicate this empathy into a captivating canvas of colors, shapes, images and typography. Your are mastering customer experiences through customer-centric designs.

Artistry is your soul, the final 21 grams in your design methodology. Your drive is the very first impressions, mesmerizing and guiding your consumers through your message and delivering that satisfying feeling, that this product is something unique, an emotional impact.

Your mind is visual and you can deliver that imagination into your work. You think in abstracts, unstructured and can turn any blank canvas into beautiful creations, without being bound by limitations.

You have a subtle mind, working the details, the nuance and esthetics. There is a deeper meaning, a soul within, transmitted into your work, carefully applied with elegance.

At a summer midnight, the music was playing and in the background, a BBC documentary was in full definition on the TV. I was alone with my thoughts, mixing colors on the wooden palate, while picking the right brush for the first stroke against the canvas, placed on the easel. This specific canvas had been through many iterations, showing character by the many layers of paint beneath.

This night was not about the picture I was about to create, masking my previous paintings in the process. This was not about the colors I was about to blend, altering the stretched cotton. This was not about picking the right brush, for that first beautiful stroke, seeing the mongoose hair, socked in colors, caressing the frame.

This was all about the moment, the feelings I had at that time, in that situation, showing my true emotions on the canvas. The light, the breeze, the temperature and the music in the room, it all came together. Unstructured and without hesitation, the brush ran through the landscape, only guided by my emotions.

I'm am an artist.

BEAUTIFUL ARTWORK

Many designers only work from the artistic point of view, thinking that design is only about art and beauty, using design as a style, only reaching the second step on the latter. These creations are not designs, they are pure artwork, valid as an artistic expression, but not as customer-centric designs.

Artwork should promote feelings and captivate the customers attention, create excitement and engagement through a carefully planned business model.

Art is when design exceeds itself and becomes more than an object, a painting or a website in the eyes of the costumer. It becomes a feeling, a memory, a fascination, a realization or an event that will linger on. Artistry is about experimentation, it's a beloved part of the designers work. It's where they set the mark of who they are and what makes their designs unique. It's this love and tenacious nature that makes designs more than just a creative idea, they becomes part of our identity.

But artistry is not the entire process, it's only the tip of the iceberg, it's the frosting on the cake. There is no formula for artistry, it's a result of who you are as a designer and what you aren't.

Being creative can be taught if you have the right mindset, but being artistic is about experience and self realization. It's about exploring the world in every possible way. It's fascination with knowledge and the unknown wonders. It's imagination and using all your senses, emotions. Open your mind and you will evolve as a designer, improving your skills. Like a musician, the ability to play more than one instrument will strengthen your understanding of notes and music.

As an artist, you celebrate different styles and explore new styles in every task. As you grow and learn through your life, you become aware of new feelings, you become older and wiser. That experience, that intelligent empathy, is told and shared through your designs.

Let me state, that beauty in design is a relative term, that doesn't imply streamlined elegance and detailed polished perfection. Beauty is in the eye of the beholder, but as we don't care about the artistic rendering of our products as a singular goal, the perception of beauty is relative to the emotional relation that our products must create.

The popular online service Craigslist is not an elegant design solution from my observation, but nevertheless resonates with their loyal customer segment, as they feel comfortable and independent by its early 80' digital design look.

Artwork is not only digital or industrial design, as artwork is in every cognitive expressions. From sound and smell, to touch and display.

In recent years, sound has emerged as an artistic expression and the way your car door sounds as it is closing, is not by default. There are many studies and insight into a luxurious expression, as the car door is closing, giving you the sense of serenity, as your are encapsulated in a beautiful silence.

At home, I have a love and hate relationship with my refrigerator from Bosch. Though they might have created many intuitive and innovative features, understanding my needs, this is sadly degraded by the emotional respond from my refrigerator. When I open the refrigerator, there is a timer activated, waiting for the door to close before an alarm is activated. This alarm is there to help me remember to close the door, which is saving both energy and preserving the food in the refrigerator. All in all a good feature.

Though this looks good and sounds good as a sales pitch, it is one of the most hated sounds in my home at the moment. When ever I forget to close the door, a nerve racking and annoying sound is beeping, reminding me to close the door, which I then do with an irritated motion. This annoying alarm sound has become a standard in many instruments and products, as the default warning sound. Though it may solve the feature, it is a great annoyance, creating emotional distance to the product, as the sound is representing a nagging product, treating you like a child.

Bosch, like many others, have created a design focusing on features, neglecting the emotions. As such, the sound is cold and careless, as it cuts through your soul each time it's activated. In contrast, my Siemens iQ tumble dryer has a different sound. Each time I start the dryer, it plays a cute little melody, a two second symphony, simply communicating, "oki-doki" as a voiceless tune. This tune makes me feel good about starting the product and I feel an emotional bond as I begin to load the dryer. It's a simple thing, but as a customer, I can relate to it.

Artwork is about expressing feelings in every format available, through sound, display, taste, smell or touch. As an artist, you must therefor understand your customers emotional reactions to each of these cognitive artworks. If you don't understand the emotions your artwork brings, then your artwork becomes careless or meaningless, as art is an expression of feelings.

CHAPTER 2

CHALLENGE

“Design is a road of obstacles,
in search of questions.”

There is a mentality, a tabu of the unknown. We are expected to be perfect, being competent and successful. We are managed and measured by our key performance indicators, in order to evaluate our success. But within these expectations, we forget that in order to learn, we must fail. In order to deliver achievements, we must first overcome challenges.

Challenges in design is a landscape of lose knots and questions, in disparate need of order. It’s important to ask questions, but it’s not always an easy task to ask the right questions.

The challenges in design will explain the questions that you need to ask, in your work and in your team, the critical thinking, defining the why. Designers are not always fond of critical thinking, conflicting with a creative and unrestricted artistic mind. But as design must be restricted to serve the customer and their circumstances, these borders must be explored through challenges.

The principles of design challenges are,

1. **Strategy**, defining what you could do. Design must be critical, asking why, uncovering the truth even when it hurts. To choose a strategy, you must know what is possible. Business is the driver for your design and your customers, thus must your work be business driven. When you ask questions, you broaden your horizon, thus expanding your view. It is important to understand what to do and what not to do.
2. **Operation**, defining what you must do. Design must be measured, learning from previous mistakes and evolve with customer feedback. Design must be based on a customer-centric pillar of data and categorization.
3. **Tactic**, defining what you should do. Design must be analytical and adaptable. You must find the most viable path for your product, through shortcuts and optimizations, creating a product framework. Without it, your products are not going to adapt to the circumstances and market demands, as every task will be difficult and unmanageable.

With an intuitive framework in place, your product has a dynamic foundation for adapting to the changing needs of your customers.

4. **Creation**, defining what you will do. Design must be experimental, lean and agile. Proving your product in early prototypes will quickly evaluate and mature your designs. Reuse your work and streamline your efforts through product components. It is important to minimize redundancy and optimize efforts, as you must reuse all thoughts and design. This will help your customers with familiarity and your production with efficiency, reducing trials and errors.

The important difference between approaching challenges in contrast to achievements, is that a challenge is a concern, a speculation, where an achievement is a desire, a specification. You could argue that it is the same thing, a task, but it is important to recognize the mindset behind the two approaches.

When you challenge yourself, you must understand the battle ground and the multiple solutions of the challenge task. Completing the challenge, is the achievement task. As a designer, you can't 'just' assume that your achievements will work, you must challenge them before moving forward.

Drawing similarities from the theory of evolution; giving a criteria such as target group, culture, functionality, communication or media; a blank canvas will evolve into a perfect adapted solution, in the hands of a designer.

Changing a criteria, could invalidate the entire design and the work will have to further evolve and adapt, just as the designer will adapt to the criteria. Challenges is about understanding the environment that your design is inhabiting, being able to survive its circumstances.

Each question will enlighten your horizon, starting from the unknown shadows. As you search for the borders of your canvas, challenges will emerge from every corner. Each challenge, each question defined, will shape your border, your canvas. As you start to understand your playground, you will understand your possibilities. Without asking questions, you will never know what could have been or what should have been. You must be curious about the product possibilities and restraints, as it will define your challenges.

Creating designs on achievements alone, is a gamble, hoping to get the answers right to a question you don't know.

A common problem arise, when designs are not targeted the customer, but instead, the client or executive management commissioning the work. This scenario creates conflicts in the entire progressive design PD° process and is a common problem for any designer.

The client or management needs to approve the work, but doesn't understand the process and is inexperienced or opinionated, lacking common knowledge about the designers advanced perception and experience. This can easily lead to my first statement; design is not a matter of taste and is not created by a committee. The client or management needs to understand that they might not like what they see, because they might not fall into the criteria for the design which is targeted the customer, not the client or executive management.

Working together in this process will insure the end result and teaching the client or management in every step, is part of the process, giving the client or management faith in the advanced skill-set of the designer who must understand the mindset of the customer.

The customer will need product satisfaction and the client or management will need concept satisfaction.

NORMALIZED QUESTIONS

Our brain have a tendency to normalize the why, the question. The less questions and answers, the less hassle we go through. We rule our day with routines and optimized processes. We don't like obstacles, we don't like questions, because we don't like the lack of answers. We get frustrated and stressed as our inbox overwhelm our attention with questions.

Standardized and public opinions becomes shared unquestionable information. We assume the facts, we trust them because they resonate with our emotions. We value social answers without judging the truth. We skim trough the daily industry news as scientific facts, written and rewritten pocket philosophies. We watch podcasts and convey their message as the gospel. We read books and magazines, without questioning the words.

Our brain process information by accepting it as the truth, avoiding the obstacles, avoiding the why. When we avoid this important aspect, we avoid going deeper and discover the details, we become superficial and our ideology becomes hollow.

A design student of mine asked the why, "Why is the green color so calming?".

"It is only calm, because you believe it is calm!", I replied, without sounding like Morpheus from the movie Matrix.

He then kept going, uncovering new layers in his question, "Why do I believe it is calm?",

"Because all your emotional relation with this color have been positive and calming", I replied.

He was on a roll and went on, "Why?".

"Because most people have the same believe as you, that the green color is calming, therefore all marketing is created with this believe and the cycle continues".

Sakichi Toyoda, defined the theory of Five Whys, an iterative question technique to seek the cause-and-effect of a particular problem. By repeatedly asking why to the answer you receive, you'll find the root answer to your initial question.

We don't ask the why, when we lack the imagination to ask the question and the confidence to seek the answer. Children master the why, because they exceed in confidence and imagination, not constraint by the adulthood reality, the negative code of behavior. We must let our questions be heard, we must let go of the tabu and seek the answer, not worrying about our intellectual perception when we ask the question.

Our most accomplished explorers and innovators have had the strength and self confidence to seek the answers and go beyond. They defied the social stigmatism and went through the unknown, filling their brain with puzzle pieces, raising up and above the answers, completing the picture and evolving our human understanding.

"Why is our web-service suddenly not working?" , I asked at an emergency meeting, chasing the root cause .

"The javascript library seams broken", an engineer replied.

"Why?", I asked.

"Our edge-server isn't delivering the static files", an architect replied.

"Why?", I asked again.

"Our account seams to be suspended", he replied.

"Why?", I asked again.

"Our credit card was declined, do to VISA requirements on our maximum monthly spending", he replied after a bit of research.

This was a bitter-sweet fault, as I didn't account for the extreme amount of traffic, that our service had gained through its sudden success. Because I had neglected to challenge the data traffic, I didn't question the server capabilities, thus failing to answer the financial achievement.

Dig into the details and simply ask why. In order to overcome challenges, you must ask the right questions, seeking the root cause.

THE EUREKA MOMENT

We all have it, that feeling that you just know the answer. We don't think about it, it's just there, written in your words, effortlessly spoken, wrapped in an assumption that this will resonate with your audience as loud as in your head. It came to your inner attention as easy as the air you breath and as such, you assume that it will resonate with your peers with the same ease. Your knowledge is shaping your mind and you must be able to communicate the vectors.

When the pieces fall together, when the puzzle becomes the single undoubtedly picture, when your knowledge becomes at the tip of your tongue, manifested in routines, executed without friction, then you have a basis for growing, bringing your knowledge towards the extreme, the intuition.

When the intuitive picture becomes the big piece and that piece becomes part of the bigger picture, epiphanies starts to emerge. Epiphanies is a state of mind where the dots suddenly connects and the picture becomes clear as the sun, highlighting the path, the truth. Eureka!

Connecting the dots will bring you closer to your epiphanies, building on your strong and undisputed knowledge, your intuition. But this state of mind doesn't come cheap, it takes on an average of ten-thousand hours for knowledge to become intuition.

Reaching an epiphany, seeing the bigger picture, is like a mental orgasm, energizing your thoughts and visions. True insight is not only about analyzing and studying the market, it's about accumulating knowledge, connecting the dots, expanding your insight as you find the hidden secrets. Let your mind become a databank of previous success and failures, creating a guideline through obstacles.

You might have felt alone with your thoughts, unable to find a colleague to share your perception with as they can't relate to your logic, while you start to questioning your own intelligence. You might wonder if it's you or them who can't comprehend the logic in what you see and are eager to share. You start to questioning the validity yourself as you seem to be the only one, who has these thoughts.

The reality is, that most people don't question the status quo and most people don't question logic. While intelligence is a relative concept, the epiphany has been a journey of thoughts that has taking you through hours of wondering, driving down the road of choices. This journey and the resulting epiphany, will not be an easy solution to translate, as people might need to get to the same epiphany on their own, reconstructing your path and result.

Ranging on the standard IQ scale, only 2% of your colleagues will have a superior intelligence and only 0.1% will be exceptionally gifted. In an organization with 1000 employees, that 0.1% could be you alone, while the superior intelligence only counts 20 colleagues. That's not a lot of intelligence, to share your gifted thoughts with.

While you might reach the eureka, feeling ecstatic and eager to share your newly discovered revolution, you could potentially hit a hard wall of disappointment, when you feel unable to share with colleagues who can understand you. Many gifted people feel alone with their thoughts and channel their dialog inward, often expressed while talking to them self. This is not an eccentric behavior, as they simply try to subject their thoughts to a basic human need, to communicate and be understood.

Challenges will demand a critical standpoint, that you question everything and always search for a better solutions, while keeping a focus on the purpose at hand. Your challenges will open your mind and explore the products true possibilities, as you must know what to do, what not to do and what to consider for the future. While an achievement is about succeeding, a challenge is a moment of reflection, pondering over your choices.

SECTION 1

STRATEGY

Strategy, defining what you could do. Design must be critical, asking why, uncovering the truth even when it hurts. To choose a strategy, you must know what is possible from customers, markets, networks and production.

Strategy is a brainstorm on the unknown, finding the gems, the opportunities, the stars and adding them to the night sky, enlighten your creativity and sparking ingenuity.

If you start your ideas with the sentence, "We just need to...", then stop and rephrase your sentence into a constructive idea. There is nothing 'just' in business design, as everything is complex and attentive work.

Strategies are merely assumptions and must be thoroughly tested as a viable path. Get out and research the street and the customers real situations. Don't assume to know, as this leads you to vanity products, only serving your assumptions and your ego.

When a new product opportunity is taking form at Bang & Olufsen, my initial work is to define the canvas between colleagues, retail stores and customers, analyzing their restraints and desires. My colleagues will challenge the feasibility, the retail stores will challenge the salability and the customers will challenge the usability. They will all add to the equation and broaden my horizon, knowing what I could do in each concept process.

Marketing strategies and business creation often react to low sales figures, trying to raise certain areas of the product offerings, solving a business problem. But if that's what everyone is doing, how do you stay ahead of the game, how do you go further, solving the reason to the problem.

You reach out and analyze the next upcoming problem, the hidden market vacuum, thereby solving it before it occurs and becomes obvious to everyone else. If you always wait for the problem to reach your doorstep, you will always be behind, playing the passive strategies. Study your customers, anticipate the next trend, behavior, need or demand. Build your strategy on real insight in the market, be aggressive and find the true strategy, not the obvious strategy to a problem that found you.

This is not as easy as written, but an essential task for your organization. Allocate the resources and time to get the needed insight to fuel your creative teams with opportunities and answers, instead of sending them into a false calculation of success.

While searching for a vacuum, it is important to understand the forces surrounding your next move. You might think that you have created a product with a true innovative edge, one that all your competitors have overlooked and neglected to incorporate in their offerings. This edge, can quickly dilute the vacuum, when you bring it to the market and the competition quickly shift and update their offerings.

Ideas are easy, even easier to replicate. While your company might have found or invented this idea, the market will quickly adjust to the demand and undermine your product, as the sustaining products from the competition will always have a higher momentum than yours.

In such circumstance, you need to define your product as a new market disruption, capitalizing on your investment as long as the product holds its stand against the emerging implosion of the vacuum. Simple services and apps are born every day, bringing new ideas and solutions to the market in small quantities, fulfilling a circumstance, a desire. While these startup apps i.a., are deployed into a vacuum, they only serve as a free experiment for the establishment, who can pursue the results as new product opportunities.

As a startup or an entrepreneuring company, you must define your explosion and implosion strategy for your vacuum product. As your explosion is the initial launch, the implosion is your next move, as you have obtained all possible outcome from the vacuum as it is imploding.

Your initial launch must catch as much territory as possible, play on all angles, while using customer emotions, as the only transferrable value from vacuum to vacuum. Ones the vacuum is gone, the disruptive product becomes a sustaining product, competing against the competition. This is often where entrepreneurs fail, as their initial strategy was build on the assumption; that their product was unique and would continue to act as a disruptive product, unable to update and follow the sustaining market.

Your implosion strategy is to either find the next vacuum and transfer the customers emotions from previous, creating a stronger product by each move, or, to stay in the game, competing on a sustaining battlefield with all your competitors. On the latter option, progressive design [PD°] principles and lean development will give you a sensier advantage, when you must create an agile and strong company structure, delivering fast and effective design solutions. As the vacuum is gone, new strategies must adapt to the new market and the fierce competition.

OPPORTUNITY PROCESS

Opportunity processes often fail, as the ability to drive new disruptive products through a mature company, is going against the very nature and business strategy of most established organizations, seeking optimized mass production.

One-size-fits-all strategies rarely works, as your organization must be capable of both sustaining and disruptive product potentials. These potentials, driven by an opportunity process, rarely fit into the sustaining process, as it is build for optimized production with less abstraction. The opportunity process is both disruptive to the market and to the organization, thus must the organization be able to handle the internal opportunities as a separate business unit, managing the abstractive behavior and innovative needs. Opportunity processes must focus on the product and the assigned team creating the product, as it will demand a more agile and creative process dealing with the unavoidable trials and errors. If the product succeeds on the market, the sustaining teams must adopt the product, streamlining its new sustaining categorization, while the disruptive teams moves on to the next opportunity.

Disruptive products, evolving through lean development, must be adopted by the sustaining teams, when they succeed. They will require operations for allowing the disruptive process to bubble up and shift into the sustaining process. As the process adopt the innovation and learnings, the process will evolve as a result of this merger.

The merger can also be a result of acquiring the disruption from other companies, as they have proven to succeed. Again, it is important not to let the disruptive product fall into normalization, as both the disruptive and the sustaining process must adapt to each other, as they must learn from each other. The disruptive product must become mainstream, while the sustaining process must evolve with the new product, getting ready for the next adoption.

Most designers see their products as children, and as such, you can draw a similarity. Each child is nurtured by its parents, like a product is nurtured by its design team, growing and learning by the process. When the children hit their teenage years, they will test all boundaries at home and in public, as they will adapt to their possibilities and restraints. When the children has found their market tier, reaching maturity, they will enter their adulthood on a sustaining path. Like the child analogy, disruptive products must be nurtured by its parents, until they reach maturity and can be adopted by the sustaining processes. As children, specific strategies and methods applies to their chaotic and disruptive nature. When they reach maturity, the sustaining strategies and methods will balance the product into mainstream production. This continued loop of new disruptive children, growing into sustaining maturity, will keep the company at float with new market opportunities, while maintaining the status quo of their current market tier with their mainstream products.

The disruptive products will reach the trend setters and early mainstreamers, while the sustaining products will reach the late mainstreamers and conservatives, produced by separate business units, operating independent on marketing and production. If the company is incapable of separating its sustaining and disruptive strategies and production, outsourcing the disruptive products to known innovators, can be beneficial.

The word product, especially as a strategy, refers to all types of customer offerings, which can be services, digital applications, physical products or components of products. Components or elements of your product, are always competing on the ability to sustain or disrupt, depending on your market. If the component is sustaining a good enough market, then outsourcing or frameworking is the preferred option, while a not good enough market will create a disruptive demand for new innovations or offerings.

INVESTING IN DESIGN

Though it is hard to quantify emotions and measure their values, history and research have defined their ROI by results.

In a 2003 research among 1,000 companies, the Danish Design Center found a 22% growth turnover in companies who'd invested in design, compared to those located at the bottom of the design latter. As the investment was significantly increased, so would the company growth, of up to 40%.

In a 2005 research, the Research Institute of the Finnish Economy examined the value of design, through success of national economics and individual companies. Through quantitative methods, they investigated wether companies who invested heavily in design could perform better, than those who hadn't. A panel of experts, used key figures to conclude, that companies who'd invested in design, had a higher sales growth and product export shares in the market.

In a 2007 survey among 1,500 participants, the UK Design Council researched the turnover of design alert businesses, which grew by an average of GBP 225 for each GBP 100 invested in design.

The survey looked at how the companies added meaningful value to their product line.

Their are multiple methods for calculating your design value within market share revenue and product categories, based on your design investment and profit, accounting multiple factors such as patents.

Long-term monitoring carried out by the red dot institute for advanced design studies, has shown that companies which invest in innovative and well-designed products in the long-term and use design as a strategic leadership instrument, often achieve above-average profit and sales figures as well as clear advantages over competitors.

SECTION 2

OPERATION

Operation, defining what you must do. Design must be measured, learning from previous mistakes and evolve with data and customer feedback. Design must be based on a customer-centric pillar of data and categorization.

As your strategic sky has enlighten your creativity, your operational mind, must find the best viable stars, the ones within grasp and the ones solving customer circumstantial needs.

You do not know what will work as an entrepreneur and most fail chasing the initial strategy, instead of learning and adjusting accordingly. Most companies succeed on strategies different to the founding strategy, as the company adapt to the dynamic circumstances of their customers. Theories and strategies, must be a dynamic definition, creating an elastic structure from the circumstances they aim to invest in.

Don't force your strategy upon your customers, let is evolve. Customers might hint of their desires and circumstantial needs, combined with the product strategy and vision, will be synthesized into achievements. Don't force your customers into your way of thinking, but instead, embrace their feedback as symbolic flaws in your design.

Though each feedback is valid, it should never be interpreted literally, as most feedbacks are simply the result of an underlaying problem.

While working with SONY® on their extranet solution, they received complains from employees on their e-learning funnel. Through the funnel and each stage, the user would supply information page by page. As the user reached the final pages, they began to worry and doubt the information they gave on the initial pages, as they started to forget what they wrote.

"Employees would like to have a summary page before submitting the final information", was the clear message from human research.

Though that would have fixed the employees doubt, it would just add to the underlaying problem, that there where simply to many unnecessary pages. I removed the pages, fiercely reducing the funnel into a single page, so the employees could gain the overview they needed, while still achieving the goal. Additionally, the company increased their e-learning completions and employee loyalty. Each user action is a potential bounce, thus by reducing the actions needed, the bounce rate decreased.

THE RUBBER BAND

What is customer loyalty, what makes your products more tied to your target and what is driving them away?

Most people in an organization can quickly answer these questions with some memorized phrases and core believes, that they feel is the fundamental difference in their offerings, compared to the competition.

Finding the true answers to loyalty, lies in a rubber band, where four forces coexists. On each sides, pulling in opposite directions, competition and dissatisfaction tries to rip the rubber band apart, while strength and elasticity is keeping the rubber band intact.

1. **Competition**, is created by the believes and offerings by the competing brands, luring the customer with promises of bigger and better. The competition can influence both strength and believe, by shifting the customers knowledge and emotions, offering better solutions and easing the burden of moving from one brand to another, with care-free packages.
2. **Dissatisfaction**, is created from broken promises and failed use-cases.
3. **Strength**, is created from the customers invested time, organizational politics, accumulating data and administrative work.

4. **Elasticity**, is created from the brand, the values and emotions that the customer has in the company and the product believe.

In order to understand to state of the rubber band, we must understand and analyze the four forces.

ANALYZING DATA

You can't judge the results of a process. You must judge the process itself. To understand a result, your must know how it came into existence. If you rely on data, calculated on the result of sales figures or trends, your study is blind to what you are truly seeking, understanding how the result came to be. You don't really care about the fire, as your focus should be on the root cause, how the fire ignited.

Working with data analyses, often holds a focus on the nearest data, not the root cause.

"Don't watch the car in front of you, watch the car in front of the car in front of you", my driving instructor rigorously repeated.

His words beautifully symbolizes the act of being one step ahead of the result. If I had to wait for the car in front of me, to react on any irregularity, it might be to late to do anything about it.

A friend of mine owns a gallery in the outskirts of the city. The gallery wasn't doing that great, which was a puzzle to him, as it had a lot of potential, if only he could improve his sales. My friend went to his receptionist, asking, “how many paintings have you sold today?”.

"Only two, today", she replied.

"How many people have been visiting", he asked.

"I don't know, we don't count that", she answered.

The next day, after implementing a daily visit count on a simple piece of paper, he asked again, “how many visits did we have today?". She replied, that 11 people visited the gallery with 2 successful purchases, a 0.18 conversion rate. The data started to grow day by day, as he could see the trend, saturday being the most successful day of the week and monday the worst. He changed his working hours to focus on saturdays, while closing the shop on mondays.

After several weeks, he went to his receptionist again, “how many people today?”, he asked.

“Nine”, she replied.

“How many people went by the gallery outside?”, he asked.

“I don’t know, we don’t count that”, she replied.

The next day, after implementing a walk-by count on a simple piece of paper, he asked once again, “how many people walked by?”. The receptionist told him, that 651 people have walked by the galleries windows, 12 entered the shop and 1 purchased a painting.

The data kept growing, analyzing further and further, but he didn’t realize the mistake he made, as he only kept his focus on the car in front of him. While analyzing the data, based on previous data, he neglected to discover two important pitfalls, that I helped him discover. First, the highest walk-by count proved to be Mondays, but as he closed the gallery on Mondays, this data was undisclosed. Second, the most important information was not analyzing data, as that is fairly straightforward, almost rhetorical, but analyzing the people who visited and their situational desires.

This is when he got a shocking fact, the initial mistake he made when requiring the data, realizing that almost all the daily visits was with the intend to purchase a painting, but as the receptionist was more eye candy than any kind of help, they walked out, empty handed. He then fired the receptionist, implemented him self as the host of the gallery, welcoming all visitors with open arms. This made a huge turnaround, as he liberated a fixed monthly salary, while selling more paintings per person and improving the conversion rate to 0.9. He had a trustful knowledge and a believable charisma, which resonated with the visitors, who where already in a state of purchase.

If your previous products have reached the critics, the fans, the trendsetters, the mainstream, the young and the old, then there is an incredible amount of research to be done now and you must be as tolerant as ever before. You will learn that your product is unusable, untested, unappealing and unsellable. You will learn that your product is fantastic, beautiful, thoughtful and a great ROI. You will learn that there is an opposite side to all your market reactions, and that the positive will only server your ego, confidence and sharpen your achievements, but the negative will be your true learnings, the feedback that can validate your challenges and polish your next release cycle.

Working with Coca-Cola® on their RedZone universe, would prove to stay sceptic about the data from the campaign. It was an aggressive strategy to turn every opportunity, within a short timespan, into a visitor. My focus was to create a well designed campaign, where we optimized every pixel available on the channels in the strategy. As the campaign started to accumulate data and we got the initial insight, the first impressions where positive, with a lot of excited feedback from both Coca-Cola® and the account managers.

This news gave every stake holder the confidence they where seeking, shifting their attention to other interests, while letting the campaign on its own. But as a designer, I didn't care for the positive news, as I knew there will always be something positive to find, if that is what you are looking for.

I started to analyze the data from the bottom up, finding the critical results and weak areas. This revealed that we could improve the campaign further, as most of our visitors where men in the age range 18-35. By segmenting the design into an older version for the men, and a completely different female version, also for two age groups, we jumped from a 5.3% visiting rate, to 13.8%. The cost of my detail attentive work, was unnoticeable by the conversion rate from the vastly improved visitors, thus creating a greater success than initially accepted.

THE MANAGEMENT DILEMMA

Product management has a tendency to focus on customer purchase at a statistical level, quantifying mass market data into a category based decisions, instead of following the thread of decisions back to the initial situation, that prompted a desired need from a customer circumstance.

Your job might be to sell me a product or service, which is resulting in massive research and marketing campaigns towards my desire for this specific product. But my desire is never the product itself, though I, as a consumer, might think that too. But a train of emotions and thoughts have lead me to a final decision, "I need your product".

Because of this dilemma, many companies have created categories based on the resulting products, lead by product managers, who aim to sustain the innovation of these categories. While the product itself is only a manifestation of one result, we neglect the possibilities of other outcomes, the neighboring opportunities. We then become blind to the real customers and the real data, unable to analyze and understand our target audience, as we focus on the fire, not the source of ignition.

SECTION 3

TACTIC

Tactic, defining what you should do. Design must be analytical and adaptable. As your strategic stars have been added to the night sky and your operation has highlighted a select few, it's now time to connect the best viable and paint the constellation.

Knowing you ups and downs, gives you the time to calculate your trajectory and investment. Your tactics is a battle plan and will define your economical and resource challenges.

Working with low budget projects, the important tactics to success; is the right platform to gain traction, the ability to reuse previous work and initial guerrilla tactics. Being able to quickly prototype and work out the conceptual ideas, before they hit the development floor is crucial to breaking ground.

Guerrilla developers are quick and skilled developers with a creative inner child, expressed through easy, no-nonsense and rule-breaking warfare. They are literally going to war and each obstacle is a quick and dirty battle by eliminating problems with smart and effective solutions tailored for the win. These battle-win-learnings are then synthesized and put into the govern development process and future concepts.

Choosing platforms and frameworks through the guerrilla process will quickly pinpoint the weak and tough areas, and which to put forward for valid and thorough business development. Guerrillas will quickly access the weak areas and address the problems ahead, giving the project a stronger and quicker starting point.

MINIMUM VIABLE PRODUCT

Great ideas are usually in plenty of supply for versioning your product, prolonging your product lifetime, but the real strategy is knowing what ideas to cut and save for later.

Consumers are not always ready for what you have to say. If your features are to young, try to implement them gradually, let them mature, without the product looking incomplete. You might think it's a great idea, but if you miscalculated the market, it can kill the product instead. Remember that you can teach your customers through iterations, implementing the longterm functionality in small batches, teaching and maturing your customers in each step.

If you implement your longterm features gradually, you can follow the customers reactions and adjust the details in each new version, creating a stronger a more reliable result through a lean production process.

Frank Robinson defined the term Minimum Viable Product or MVP, as a practice of small batch development in lean manufacturing. When you focus on the core features, releasing to a subset of customers, you achieve the ability to experiment and adjust accordingly, quickly fine-tuning your product, in each iteration. As speed-to-market is important with sustaining products, being part of the market share game, a short and quick iteration cycle is needed, being leaner and faster than the competitors.

Because you build your products on a story, your design will always have a personality, a soul that communicate this story through your design language, regardless of the missing features in your MVP.

Turner, the broadcasting organization behind CNN, TNT, adult swim and other beloved TV channels, where battling the decision to be part of the maturing video on-demand market. Grasping their market share, without losing or dilute the carefully established broadcasting offer, was crucial. While many are emerging on this new territory, spearheaded by the disruptive Netflix, who has establish themselves as a sustaining broadcaster, it could seem impossible to be part of, if your feel a bit late to the party. But as the market shares are now build on sustaining technology, there is no hindrance to grasp, what is there for the taking.

As the market shares and the ability to stay in the game is based on simple clever marketing and architecture, not emotions, you simply need to design your game strategy, competing on the metrics.

While working with Turner as a consultant, I designed a shortcut to kickstart their on-demand adventure, competing with Netflix as a platform. Grasping the development as a cross-device tactic, releasing simultaneous to both desktop, television, mobile and tablet platforms, with low management and cost sustainability, proved vital for raising the approval for the project.

Many organizations are afraid of jumping into such jungles as they might loose footing on their current path, investing in heavy and unadaptable architecture, failing to bring the tactic together with marketing, who might be a separate entity within the organization. Such a tactic must be build on theory, where all entities are incorporated and each explored to find the shortcuts.

LESS IS NOT ALWAYS MORE

Simplicity is not just a visual concept, woven into the job titles of information architects and experience designers. Simplicity is the art of removing clutter and redundancy in all areas of your design process, even production.

“I have never seen an engineer as lazy as you. That makes you my most talented employee”, said a former employer of mine.

His words reminded me, that the work of simplicity, can quickly be seen as lazy behavior, as the goal is to do as little as possible. Though he knew that my work was the best he had seen, he often joked about the parallels. As a design engineer, my focus was constantly on optimizing my workflow, producing faster results, with higher quality and reliability.

Working with one of the leading travel agencies, I designed a new portal for customers to create road-trip bookings. This required that the customers could add their start, stop and intermediate destinations into the portal. The architects on the project had worked on multiple workflows during our design stages, but had focused to much on the visual part of the flow. The results was two separate screens, with start and stop destinations on the first, and optional intermediate destinations on the second screen. This was created from the theory, less-is-more, working with simplicity as user interaction stages.

Less is more, but only when it is truly less. Since this is rarely the case, less can quickly become less, when the simplicity is superficial or misguided. The user in this scenario would have to enter his or hers start and stop destination, then move on to the next screen, loosing the references of the first screen. On the second screen, the user would have to gain yet another overview of the screen, as the content has changed. In this scenario, less is less, as the reference is lost, when it is needed, confusing the user. By combining the two screens, adding an optional intermediate destination button, that would insert new destination into the travel plan, would create a greater overview and comfort for the user, reducing stress. As progressive interaction yields a higher level of overview and comfort for the user, the strategy creates a higher level of success and loyalty from the users.

Progressive interaction was not my only thought, when I suggested to combine the screens, as I also had the system architecture and management resources in mind. By creating two screens, this would also create two sets of controls in the system, which doesn't sound like much extra work.

The additional screen creates one more screen to test, one more screen to debug, one more screen to layout, on more screen to approve, on more screen to adjust, one more screen to fail, one more screen to document, one more screen to project manage, one more screen to ticket.

Simplicity isn't just about user interactions, it's just as important under the hood, throughout the entire project. Combining the interaction strategy with system architecture, will reduce cost and resources, by creating a better, quicker and more efficient product, that both user, stakeholders and deadlines will benefit from.

Tactic in design, is the ability to choose the right framework, limiting your obstacles by achieving a standardized, yet adaptable solution. A tactic is to find the shortcut that will give you the better hand, building upon the knowledge of possibilities and limitations, calculating the best viable outcome.

SECTION 4

CREATION

Creation, defining what you will do. Design must be experimental, lean and agile. As the constellation has been aligned, the connected stars form a shallow line, missing an artistic expression, creating the true understanding. Your creational phase will define the skin on the bones and muscles, the curves and contrast.

Ensuring innovation, validation and cost efficient development of products, productive prototyping is the key to design creation. Ideas are easy to get, easy to misunderstand and easy to love as long as they are part of your intangible imagination. As soon as your ideas becomes tangible in the shape of a prototype, the reality starts to define the merits of your ideas. Make sure that meetings, alignments and workshops are based on tangible and understandable prototypes.

Prototyping ideas and exploring the possibility of structures, is vital for any growth. The secret to innovation is finding hidden treasures in the industry, little sparks of pure genius, often overseen by irrelevance or lack of knowledge. These treasures are often found hidden within other products, as a small feature, buried by the developers unknowing of their potential. Having the ability to see through the product feature and discover the gems within, driving the innovation and marvel, can be your next building block. Having a backlog of gems is important, to be part of the next revolution or to stay ahead of the game, creating rapid solutions.

If you're lucky, there is a perfect framework available for your next project, suiting all your needs, but most likely, you're not. Researching frameworks, platforms, foundations and understanding their unique nature will give you the ability to shift components from one platform to another. This will create dynamic platforms where you can build the needed foundation, where every metric is spinning to the sound of your story, creating traction and progress, with room to expand.

Productive prototyping is a process, where prototyping is an evolving and changeable structure. It will evolve and change through the four achievements phases. Each phase carried out, will insure a shared understanding of the details. Each phase eliminated, will open the detail for interpretation. Giving no room for interpretation, will speed up the project and limit the iteration process to a minimum, minimizing cost and resources.

KNOWLEDGE EXPERIMENTS

A design experiment is a challenge of knowledge, performed when we don't know the answer or assume the outcome. As design can't be build on assumptions, we must know, discard or experiment with our proposed facts.

Experiments are often a vital part of fine-tuning products and scoping new opportunities, as we are searching for subtleties. Though experiments can't lead the design, it can play the voice of the environment. If we substitute insight, design visions and creativity for customer experimentations and data analysis, our design would be crowdsourced and based on customer feedback. Because most customers don't know what they want, they wont be able to drive the design in any visionary direction, further more, we wouldn't be able to deliver any magical moments, as we would rely on the customers imagination to get us there.

The lean startup movement is advocating build-measure-learn loops, an increasingly popular ideology. But designs relying primarily on these loops of experiments, becomes subject to quantifying data. As such, the data will only serve as results, not depicting the customers process, failing to learn the circumstantial desire. As the process is more important than the result, we must be able to follow or reverse engineer such data sets, finding the real information, why customers are using our products.

Data will only tell you about the past, but the ability to see the data patterns, will guide you to the real insight. Customers are not buying or using a product because they want an hammer, an iPhone, a B&O Television, a McDonald Coin Offer or a Netflix Movie. There is a reason for wanting these experiences, which is the initial need, that a designer must have the insight to learn.

If every feature is the ability to measure their value, then values becomes metrics and design becomes an ability to measure. Neglecting the poet and the artist in these measurements, creates stereotypic and engineered solutions, catering product to the lowest denominator. If we rely on the customers to tell us what to improve, we won't expand their knowledge, their trust, their emotions and their believes.

We must embrace the balance between measurable market demands and magical experiences, moving the customer, learning, measuring and understanding on all design principles.

Upgrader, a company providing executive management software for some of the largest enterprises in the world. They had the market demand, they had the ability to sell and they knew what they where doing, with increasing revenue and solid insight. What they didn't have, was the ability to scale and grow their system infrastructure.

Customers where nocking on their door, as they constantly added efforts to expand their company, realizing that their system software was failing, unable to repair or renew the old one, they felt stuck. Creating a new system software from scratch, of that magnitude, is not an easy nor cheap solution. Even worse, they had neither time nor resources available.

In close dialog with the managing partners, they embarked on an unknown journey with me as their enterprise designer, trusting the theory, believing in the ideology as I explained my solution.

I had a three step plan to solve their problem. We had to be smart and think outside the box. We needed to design our way out of the situation, minimizing time, cost and avoiding the problem in the future, though creating a product of higher value than what we would replace.

1st, we needed an edge, something dynamic and solid to build upon, which could drive innovation and a diverged client art direction, as each client wanted the software themed with their brand. I found the answer in a versatile and popular open-source framework, which shall remain nameless, proved to have the edge we so desperately needed. I continued my research, asking the all important why. Why was this framework so versatile and intuitive, what made it so popular? The answer was the framework within the framework, a hidden diamond, that no one had published, yet. It was like discovering a nuclear reactor within a kitchen blender.

2nd, releasing in small batches. With an impossible deadline, customer experiments would alter the final product quickly. Month after month, we released an iterated MVP, with daily minor bug updates. This quick and experimental release cycle made it possible to fix the errors week after week, quickly solving problems and responding to customer demands, polishing the functions. With the new deployment infrastructure in place, we could commit a new change to the cloud of twenty edge-servers world wide, within minutes. The next day, we could track the progress of that specific commit, measuring failures and customer feedback, monitoring the support center and talking to client representatives. We could then adjust or roll back, if the problems where too severe.

3th, after an online venture of just six months, with an overwhelming success from staff and clients, I suggested to keep the lean manufacturing running at full speed, improving everyday on the system by achieving the necessary knowledge. I secured one of the most talented engineers I have ever had the pleasure of working with, as their new Senior Web Manager, leading their production. Having the right people, gifted people, who believes in design as a business, will change your products from rocks to diamonds, keeping you resources, deadlines and cost below estimates.

With a new production in place, they started to evolve on the culture and infrastructure, that proved to drive a fast-paced development cycle, through experiments. Each experiment was released to a staging server for validation and test. A random customer account was automatically switched to this server. If the experiment was a success, the software would be released to the production server, as the new stable version. If the experiment was a failure, the random selected customer account would be reverted back to the production server, running the previous software version, while a new experiment was in the making.

Each experiment, would challenge the user on design perception, improving on interaction, new technics or functionality. An experiment was never about fixing bugs or improving the stability of the software, but always had a customer-centric approach, as stability and thorough testing is implied before any release.

Google is an organization with an immense potential for experiments, serving billions of requests on a daily basis. Choosing a small segments of users to perform an experience upon, will quickly validate the experiment, while only reflecting this upon the unsuspecting, creating a contrast against the unaffected. Through these quick and easy releases, Google has experimented with everything from functions and styles, to branding and offers. With each experiment, they can see which font style has the best outcome and what number of advertisements will serve them best. Each little detail is submitted to the customers environment, where it's survival of the fittest.

As a designer, this test will quickly polish the work you have added to the environment. Though the customers indirect feedback won't add nor subtract from your solution, it will polish the details. Experimenting on a bad solution won't make it great, as the customers don't hold a vision towards your product, but it'll iron out the wrinkles and improve on the features available.

In fashion, luxury clothing brands are often seen as trend-setters. But the reality in fashion is the level of curation, derived from the emerging experiments from designers. Independent designers, experiments on the same principles as any other industry. Each piece is added to their name, as a single shot or an entire collection, which is then tested against the industries critical society. The experiments that work, will be picked up or inspire the established store brands. The more you curate and simplify your collection, the higher your brand will be perceived as premium, targeting early mainstreamers.

Even this book started as an experiment, in the form of articles on my website at lindborg.io. As the articles started to gain followers and popularity, I started the more attentive work of writing and editing the book. As I reached a critical level of pages and balance, I published the book on Amazon and iTunes as a digital edition, even though this early version was nowhere near the version I wanted it to be. But as the sale started to grow, I could see the popularity and thus validated my next move. I doubled down on the following versions, updating the digital edition, getting feedback, editing, iterating.

As these cycles continued to improve from the feedback I received, I stepped up and created the printable layout for the book, choosing a cost effective and well renowned publishing company to deliver the first test print as a small batch prototype. This batch was then used as another level in the iteration process, to gain critic and insight into the paperback challenges, as both printing, design and marketing would start to grow in complexity, moving from the quick shifting and adaptable digital world, to the physical products of the unchangeable printed books. Even as a printed book, I kept learning and updating, changing size, paper type, layout and font with each iteration. As I never ordered more prints than I wanted to learn from, each investment would always serve as either a failure to learn or success to confirm, both equally valuable experiments.

All the way through these iterations, I reacted fast and even before I was at the level of my own personal approval, gaining insight and learnings as I progressed. This gave me the validation and comfort as I went into new and fast moving territories, without losing my investment on hopes and speculations.

Though the first editions started as experiments, they where never perceived as experiments, as the book was well intended for release and gained popularity from the first purchase, while I continue to update and edit the book in its forthcoming editions. This follows the same principles as most products on the market, like cars, televisions, mobile phones, as they are released and updated each year, with improvements to their previous learnings. The difference is the small batches and quicker iteration cycles, keeping a minimum viable product for each release that moves faster throughout the process and thus learns faster.

It is said that Thomas Edison failed school, as his teachers never perceived him as anything else than too stupid to learn, always failing in his attempts. While inventing the lightbulb, his community witnessed his attempts and failures through a thousand iterations before achieving. In their eyes, he failed miserably before getting it right. This gave rise to the quote, “I didn't fail a thousand times, I learned a thousand ways not to make a lightbulb”.

Failures and learnings are the same thing, though our society don't always see it that way.

CHAPTER 3

ACHIEVE

"Design is within opportunities, discovering the answers."

Achievements in design, is the answers you will find to your questions, the forward-moving creative thinking. By each achievement, your product will define its substance, as each achievement will define the how, layer by layer.

The principles of design achievements are,

1. **Story**, the users desires. Design must have a resonating and coherent concept. Story is the hunt for new knowledge, searching for vacuums to explore, always seeking the answers to your business goals. A story marvels a users desire for

meaning, finding the unknown insight to their product circumstances. At the hearth of your product is the true insight to success, understanding the customers desires.

2. **Function**, the users needs. Design must be useful and solve a users need to achieve an obstacle through the story. The function is giving substance to the story, supporting the weight as a skeleton.

3. **Journey**, the users behaviors. Design must anticipate the users actions and reactions, the mental process of elaborating on what you already know to be true, extending you horizon. A journey creates meaning to the function, as it can be applied to the users circumstances, adding flexibility, i.e. product muscles.

4. **Expression**, the product bond. Design must be orchestrated, directed as beautiful artwork, an emotional symphony. Expressions are the intangible embodiment of the emotional relationship with the user. An expression fuels a users emotional relationship throughout the journey, applied as the exterior skin.

Design is achievements, answers and opportunities scoped from story and function to journey and expression. Design is more than popular opinions, art direction and outdated design manuals. It's the story before function, function before journey and journey before expression. This is an important process from a production standpoint. From a users standpoint, it's the opposite direction, starting with the experience, as this is the first encounter. This is what many designers misinterprets, as this is how they themselves perceive design.

Analyzing your needed achievement outcome, must be a combination of customer story, function, journey and experience. Four distinct achievements, that will lead you to open your horizon while keeping focus. Choosing only a few of these achievements, will limit you potential within the product design, limiting the ability to gain trust and believe from your customers.

Being a designer is, at the core, about story and functionality, not artwork. Artwork is the exciting experience and the attention parameter for all of us, bonding with an emotional relation. It's what we as costumers are attracted to. But when the first impressions are over, the attention is moving and the costumer is fulfilled. Now the design has to deliver more than just first impressions, it has to have a great function, a use, a purpose and it has to meet the users expectations beyond artwork.

If you don't want your design to end up in the back of the costumers mind, it has to be functional, it has to enrich your users with new possibilities, it has to be more than just pretty, you must think like a designer, not a costumer.

It should follow the user and be as simple as the breeze, functionality that become silent and unnoticeable. Pretty is easy, but innovative compelling functionality, with exciting emotional possibilities, is not for the faint of hearth.

When you envision a product, you start with the story, the functionality, then structure and in the end, artwork. Designs and designers focusing on artwork before story, function and journey, are designing glass hammers, it might be beautiful, but not very practical.

Story will define the product essence, functionality will make the product sustainable, a structured journey will give the product usability and the experience will satisfy the user, communicating emotional quality and brand values.

Search your true poetic center, your focus, find the simplistic and true concept for your product, the signature experience, following your design language and story. When you know what will make this product unique and resonate, you can define the functionality, the technical need and sustainability, as an engineer, the very core mechanics of your product. When you know what your product can achieve as a concept, as a technical solution, you have a platform to build on, you have defined the essence of your product. You will then shape and bend your functionality, into a user journey as an architect, streamlining every metric, reducing redundancy and understanding the bigger picture. In the end, you will unleash your artist and sculpt the impressions of the product, the very soul and personality, that must accomplish consumer admiration and become more than a product, it'll be an experience.

Design is about the engine, before the chassis. Imagine you've purchased a car with all the right curves, simply a work of art. But then you take a look at the engine; it's small, it's limited and it is far from the spirit of the products design. There is a gap between the two things, unmatched expectations. The product is beautiful on the outside, but falling apart on the inside. The functionality of the product is not what you would expect as a customer and you end up with a sense that your product is fake, it's hollow, it's missing its core, the functionality, the possibilities.

The brand becomes shallow and you distance yourself from it's values, as you know each sentence and promise is a lie.

While working with Maersk, one of the biggest shipping companies in the world, we envisioned a project that would create a deeper understanding of the Maersk brand, targeting the employees.

Through interactive games, the employees where questioned and competing in a jeopardy show, challenging their pop quiz skills against their colleagues, while creating an emotional bond with fun and animated theatrics. Though the theatrics was an easy stunt to get the first excitement going, the game needed a journey, guiding the user through the experience, aligning expectations.

The journey was a symphony of storytelling and actions, combining their strong heritage with the games experience, moving the journey along. While the journey would keep aligning expectations with experience, the game needed a valid function, proving its purpose.

The game felt responsive and reactive, as the functions where created in contrast to the employees devices and interactions, serving the story.

The story behind the game was to serve a stronger employee brand, a believe in the spirit and vision, as the worlds leading shipping company. The project was an overall employee branding challenge, where game mentality would engage the different departments, while achieving a deeper level of knowledge and shared understanding of the company they where working in.

I have explained this case from a users standpoint, starting with the experience, unraveling layer by layer. But the experience was the last element added from a design standpoint, as my first thought was the core, the story, evolving through each achievement. Starting with the story, then adding function, journey and finally user experience, building by each achievement, bringing a unique product to life from the real insights.

The original story might be respectful, but didn't resonate with the wast amount of employees on all levels, as they can't all relate the the executive floor. Many employees where excited about their job, but felt detached from the executive strategies and culture. This situation is not uncommon, as many companies struggle to evolve their executive culture to incorporate the people within it, trying to establish an executive vision, indulged in executive speech. By using this insightful knowledge, we could turn the project into a interactive game between colleagues, relating on known emotions and their peers.

With colleagues as the story, we now needed to bring that message into a framework that could support it, as multiple devices and customer behaviors would be common scenarios. The game needed to be fun and relatable, to a social and corporate culture, which drove us in the direction of a jeopardy concept.

With function in place, we needed to define the user journey. What would bring the employee through the game and make them understand the story. We used the corporate history and well defined pillars of employee values as learning curve. From these pillars we could guide the employees through the came by referencing to known objects and emotions.

With the journey in place, we now needed to define the user experience. Believe is an important user perception and your first task in creating an experience, is perceiving the employees emotional values. The game needed a social context and a bit of theatrics to lighten the mood and skepticism in the quiz. With a couple of fun character animations, beautiful and delightful backgrounds with rich motion and artwork, we could turn the first negative reactions into a state of wonder.

By using insightful learnings as the true story, the game became about friendships and social happiness, shaking the colleagues together, solving an employee circumstantial need, strengthening the workplace and culture. Though the executive strategy was to understand the employee level of knowledge, we needed to bring the story into a context, where we understood the employee and their circumstantial needs.

If I didn't care about the customer-centric design, I would have created a game based on the original brief, designing the game from a employee standpoint, starting with the experience and theatrics. That would have lead me to a ego-centric design, creating a presumptuous concept.

It is important to work with achievements in the right order, starting with the story, defining how you will solve a users circumstantial need. When you know where to start, you can begin to define the next layer, the functionality. As you know what function will serve your story, the journey will give meaning and direction to your features. In the end, the experience will make the product relatable and believable, as the user can bond with the journey, the functionality and the story, through artwork.

SECTION 1

STORY

Customers don't know why their emotions resonate with your product and often proclaim their devotion by the products functional or financial benefits instead. They speak about the signature features or how much they spend on their latest purchase, instead of why they really bought the product, the added emotional value. The ability to perceive this value, is the story you must first gain in order to build the functionality.

Because of this dilemma, production houses and organizations located at the bottom of the design latter think that customers demand the feature rich products. But when you scratch the surface, layer by layer, the real demand is the ability to understand customers circumstantial needs, the story at the core.

Customers don't need nor buy your products. Your products are just a mean to an end. Your offering is there to fix a circumstantial need, in your customers daily life and your real product is to solve that need.

People don't buy hammers, they buy the ability to get things done. People don't buy milkshakes, they buy a refreshing moment. People don't buy mobile phones, they buy connectivity. Your product story and management categorization must be build on such insights.

Understanding the business side of your product, is key to your story, asking the all important why. Studying and analyzing trends, market behaviors and consumer feedback will guide you towards the true value of your product, the unique and tangible story, that will resonate with your organization and target audience.

All questions must be asked and answered, challenged and achieved, diving into the dark unknown ocean of discovery, searching for that one key aspect, that will give you a unique market insight.

If you start your story by assuming that customers will change or your expect your customers to change to embrace your story, stop. No good have ever come from this assumption, that people just need to accept your story, as you have. These assumptions will lead startups and established companies to brake, as customers can't understand what your are implying. As a story teller, you must catch my attention from the first phrase, guide me through your story as the journey unravels and I engage your experience by each function.

Customers don't know what they want, before you show them what they want. Customers can only relate to them self and their situational desires, they will not revolutionize your products, because they don't know what story to be told. This is where the designers most important task is starting, telling the compelling, coherent and resonating story that will bond with the user through function, journey and experience.

Don't tell a story, which you don't know the ending to. It's like listening to your friends, eager to tell a joke, taking you on a roller coster ride of energetic arm gestures and acting, creating immense excitement, as they suddenly realize, they can't remember the ending.

When I dine at my favorite restaurant, I like to know that the meat is from the local area, raised in comfort and grass-fed. I like to know that I'm eating healthy and quality food, because I like to add meaning to what we eat.

When I buy a new TV, I like to know how special and unique it is, as I like to differentiate my products by luxury and features. I like to know that I'm capable of achieving premium products and that I'm surrounded by something unique, as I want these products to add meaning to my life.

We all like a good story, as it adds emotional value to what we do in the moment. These values are derived from a perceived understanding by the product, that we feel the product is achieving higher level of insight in our needs and desires. We feel that the product understands us and that our lives are better, because of this product.

USER RELATION

Creating a strong story is a creative process where all emotions are embedded into your product. Your story promotes feelings that extends the functionality and essence of the product, it becomes an object of love. We all have an understanding of love, but more important, there is a shared understanding and expected believe in the word.

Love is more than a feeling, it's the sum of all our memories, emotions and visions. Love is the history we have, tied op in strong and clear memories. It's the emotions we feel in the moment and the rich experience we have when we interact. It's our visions for the future, the believe that this will only be better, that our love will grow and strengthen our possibilities. When we love, our life is enriched and become ecstatic, when love is shattered, all that is ripped away from us, and we fell empty, broken, lost.

Just like love, a story is an explosion of values that we crave and want to be part of. It's an idea, a belonging that will evolve over time. Person, idea or object, we can fall in love with anything and that is your foundation for your story.

Make your costumer fall in love!

In 1998, Ericsson mobile phones was, in my mind, the most stylish and innovative devices on the market. Each model defined me, they satisfied my gadget cravings and demanded my attention - I just couldn't get enough of the iconic T28 and later T39. The more I used my phone, invested time and money in each model, configuring my preferences just as I needed, the more I fell in love with the brand. It was me and Ericsson forever.

In 2001, Nokia released a new device, the 8310, a model that would change everything that I thought I wanted in a phone. It was small, handy, stylish, beautiful and full of functions that I didn't need, but wanted to need - It became my new love. It was me end Nokia forever.

In 2008, Apple released a new device, the first iPhone, a model that would change everything that I thought I wanted in a phone. It was magical love from first sight. Each year would bring me closer and closer by each new iPhone i bought, until one day in 2014, when my logic overcame my devotion. The iWatch was not the Apple I knew and I started to question their vision and their brand. My emotional attachment started to drift away, as I saw them align on a mass market, falling behind, where the empathic design was replaced by a buffet table of features.

I'm an early mainstreamer in the trend diamond model. As such, I seek disruptive products as new innovations are brought forth. With the iPhone 6 and iPhone 6 Plus release, Apple is falling into the mainstream market, which doesn't resonate with me. Because of this, I started to drift away from the brand, as I began to search for the next disruption.

My beloved product is no longer the same product that I fell in love with. We only believe in the story as long as we can relate to the brand. As we grow or our circumstances change, our brand reflection change.

When you define your product story, you must be able to define the complete offer and all the intricate details, allocating budget, knowledge and resources.

SECTION 2

FUNCTION

The kitchen is my place of reflection. It is where I relax and find my center. Experimenting with food is relatively easy and you quickly discover what to do, what to improve and what to avoid. As you experiment, you realize what tools are missing, what equipments are inferior and where your weaknesses are. This is also true in design, where experimentations and the learnings thereof, will evolve you, your tools and your designs, if you study your results.

It's equally important to fail, as it is to succeed. When you fail, you learn something new, when you succeed, you strengthen what you already know.

The designer stow is increasing in popularity, covering its entire surface in glass, housing a colorful digital display and seamless touch buttons for operating the plates. This creates a beautiful exterior, removing the bulky nobs of previous designs. As you start to use the stow rigorously, you'll understand the design standard or lack there of, as this is not very practical.

With the old designs, you could simply turn a nob in one motion, with a firm grab and the flip of your hand. With the new designs, you need to press and hold the activation area, wait for it to acknowledge your action, then select your plate, then repeatedly press the plus icon to get from zero to six, indicating your level of heat. This user interaction strategy, doesn't solve a problem, it introduces one, infused in superficial surface design, design as a style. I was happy with the previous stow, though I like the look of the new stow, but my need for function and simplicity outweighs my need for beauty, as it feels fake and hollow, unaware of my needs. Even my emotions are battling this design, as I respond in favor to its beauty, but feel mislead by its functional promise, which it can't deliver.

The stow has another flaw, as the digital display and touch buttons, located on the glass surface, gets incredible hot when pans and pots covers the adjacent area. This design flaw has apparently been tested and solved with a safety function, which turns the stow off automatically. I experienced this during a christmas dinner, cooking for twelve excited and hungry guests. All plates where in use, when the stow suddenly gets to hot and for safety reasons, shuts down. After cooling the display for thirty minutes with a fan, I could continue, carefully, with my important dinner plans. This is a design based on immature technology and bad interaction observations, as the stow has been designed for style, not for customer situations or even function.

Unused or difficult functions should not be removed without further investigation from your product iterations. Customers or management might force you to remove them, but a lot of work have been put into creating that specific function and might still serve a purpose, as the answer could be lack of story, journey or experience. It could simply be, that the function should be further developed, to better serve the initial insights.

In your first version, it is natural to pay attention to the big picture, the entire product. But as you start to update your product line, some functions will begin to fall short from lack of attention. This could be perceived as missing interest from the market, or it could be that the market don't understand the specific function. In either case, you must know why and update your product accordingly.

If the market don't understand it, you need to spend more time with the function, to polish the story into better functionality, expressed through journey and experience.

If the market isn't interested, you need to know if this is in lack of knowledge, situational needs or desires. These insight might shift your product to a market on the move or find new markets.

When creating products, they must be aligned with the customers expectations and desires, created for a situational purposes. If the mainstream market is filled with products that are good enough, a pursue of offering better or more expensive products, will result in overselling to a market, that are not interested in your offerings. In such cases, the offering has to be targeted a niche segment, who look for more esoteric or luxurious brands.

Defining what is good enough in your market tier, will often result in an array of product variations, as the decision is relative to each customer segment. The mobile phone is never good enough, as we can see this by the vast amount of offerings in this industry. The amount of platforms, sizes, capabilities and accessories, competing in an shared experiment, as the customers will choose which device has the best combination of offerings. While the battery is important to most people, other value the processing speed or screen size. As the innovation evolve, the compromises will be limited and shift to new compromises. In this shared experiment, analyzing the competitors offerings and sales, will yield the customers desires of functionality.

Looking at the bloom of 3D capable televisions in the early 2010, the functionality was immature but eager to reach the customers, as the television is a sustaining innovation, evolving. As every TV brand had a 3D offer, the customers started to question their desire for 3D, "should I own such a product?". It became something to talk aout. But as the functionality was immature and the customers situational purpose was non existing, the 3D televisions became a must-have on the checklist, but a nice-to-have in the living room. Customers who bought a 3D TV, quickly realized, that the home experience was far from the cinematic experience, they where hoping to get.

This battle of offering the latest and greatest, dilute the mainstream market, as the customers are now expected to expect the offering. They had no desire, nor interest in this functionality, as it's suddenly the talk of the community. Every year, standard products are updated with better and smarter solutions, in a fast pace race to be the ultimate mainstream product, packed with an overwhelming amount of functions.

As the pursue of functionality, i.e. innovation, is important, for evolving the industry, the pursue of customer-centric products has to be the principle for putting new functions forward. Customers won't use functionality, just because it's smart or trending, though they might buy it because of that reason. In this dilemma, it has to suit a situation, where the customer wants a better solution, known or unknown to their own desires. Put your product in a contextual situation and discover what the product is really achieving.

The sustaining product is often a necessary evil, which can keep you in the game while achieving the status quo. The sustaining product is simply taking part in the unending arms raise of keeping the product aligned with the competition, often ending when small mistakes are made, which limits the sale and thus the ability to grow and follow the competitors.

Creating new product disruptions is a way of staying top-of-mind in the market, while keeping the seat warm. But these innovations or breakthroughs has to be more than just features, which will easily be duplicated by the competition. They have to move the customer into the path of trust, as the function is not just solving a problem, it is solving a desire, a means to an end.

The nordic music service Wimp, is aligned in the european market, together with Spotify, Deezer, iTunes and Google Music. It is easy to say that Spotify is ahead of the game in 2013 and you could argue that they are the best. Bet there is nothing revolutionary or emotional relatable about the company nor their app, which makes it easy and almost encourage you to try out the competition. In 2014, Google is moving into the market and provides exactly the same features, music and pricing. As Google has a lot more muscle, i.e. architecture, Spotify will now have to tread lightly, while they are now fighting on sustaining products.

The battle of sustaining products, fighting over mass market shares, is a game of poker. As long as you can buy new chips, raise or fold, you can stay in the game. When you bet or call, your strategy must guide you through these difficult and critical decisions.

Wimp is a relatively small company compared to Google, but had the fortune of acquiring audio and streaming technology, thus being part of the game. But as a small company, they will always be compared to Google, who can continuously buy new chips in bundles, thus prolonging the inevitable outcome of Wimp, betting it all and loosing. But Wimp is smarter than that and are focusing on the niche market, the loyal market shares. They are not playing the mass market game, they are playing a different game where they have a more reliable footing, creating functionality with meaning.

A meaningful function is rooted in the understanding of the users situational need, creating magic and believe, that the company understands a customers desire.

SECTION 3

JOURNEY

The user journey, from advertisement and sale, to setup and daily use, is part of the overall picture, the expectations and experiences. Your role as a designer is not just the product, because you don't design products, you design a journey and the journey start with the first knowledge about the product, building user expectations.

When you design a product, your focus is usually on the product itself, frozen in time, turning every use-case and corner-case scenarios, validating the experience. You aim for the vary highest experience, the ultimate usability, the strongest communication and the reliable interaction. You are careful about the previous fails and the learnings from your community. You build a product based on the pride and skills you have nourished so deeply through your career.

The journey must be a view of the product as a 360° experience. If you don't consider the entire product lifetime and journey, from sale to use, then your work is created in a vacuum, with a limited view.

The journey is starting when we first experience a sales poster, website advertisement or shop window. This is where you must meet the demand that soon will be your products expected delivery.

Analyzing what your customers are expecting, will deliver you more insights than anything else. You will be able to find the right level of commitment and align all your product related activities within marketing, service, production and design. You might discover that your users demand more or less of your product, while you might be working in the opposite direction, resulting in either underused or overused resources.

It's not about reaching the highest standard, it's about aligning expectations. If you sell a mainstream product, then your customers won't expect luxurious details and innovation. If you sell an expensive product, then you must deliver on those high expectations that often follows the price tag. But you control the expectations, you designed the sales poster, you communicated the website advertisement and you created the shop window. You don't design a product, you design a journey of expectations.

There is a popular saying amongst designers and developers, that "customers are stupid" and that the designer knows best. A teacher of mine ones said, there are no dumb questions, only dumb answers. Designers who implement behavioral psychology and manipulate their customers into use-cases and patterns, are creating presumptuous products, thinking that they know better. A designer will always know better, but that arrogant attitude will quickly move you towards the ego-centric design and away from the empathic customer-centric design.

Customer behaviors are not there to be changed, but instead, we must study and understand in order to inspire new products from this insight. If customers are misusing or unable to understand your products intended use, then your product journey has failed. Your customers inability to use your product as intended, is an opportunity to inspire new products from that insight or adapt the product to your customers desired behaviors.

Customer behaviors will follow the path of least resistance. Don't try to force your customers into a desired journey, simply because it fits your business model or you're unable to change your product design. Inspire or study customer behaviors, as you'll quickly lose momentum and strength going against the flow.

Don't design customers for your products, design products for your customers.

A dear friend of mine is a landscape architect, working with entrepreneurs on new buildings and public gardens. When starting on a new project, his first step is a naked foundation, a minimal solution intended for testing human behavior. From the rough terrain, he quickly sees how people walk across the naked landscape, between the adjacent points of interest. This initial learning is then added to his sketches, as he now know how to facilitate these behaviors, instead of going against it. When the pathways are established and validated, he then add the vegetation to create a rich experience.

He is well aware, that planting pathways and vegetation without this initial insight, will force the users to go against their will and the optimal path. This would quickly break his creation, as users would walk on unintended terrain, destroying the vegetation.

Because all customers are unique, they will behave in any number of ways, which will be impossible to predict. Some of these fall between two functions, an unintended behavior or use case. In such cases, we must understand why that happened, as we must know if our product is being used unintended, meaning that there might be another opportunity for your product, or are people creating shortcuts, meaning that the product is difficult to use.

CUSTOMER EXPECTATIONS

The word *customer* can be both dealer, manager, service representative, user, buyer or customer-to-customer. The customer is the person who must buy into the story, investing time and resources in the product, not necessarily the person buying the product.

An expectation is to get what you imagine you want, within a frame of thoughts. Expectations builds on the premise; I observe, I relate, I want. Expectations are created by a cognitive observation within us all, fulfilling our brain with dopamine and desires from the input we receive, driven by our reptilian urges, i.e. food, sex and other primal instincts. Each step we take towards an expectation, is an instinct to satisfy these cravings. We fuel our desire and endlessly anticipating the delivery of that desire. The journey is a series of expectations and deliveries, each creating a micro experience, building upon each other, keeping our attention and desire ongoing within the entire experience.

1. When you deliver on an expectation, the user is satisfied and at ease, slowly burning the last fuel of the delivered desire, neither approving nor disapproving the experience. In this state of mind, we won't remember the experience, neither as bad nor god, processing the experience as redundant, forgettable.
2. When you exceed an expectation, the user will be amazed, marveled by the fact that there is more to the expectation than imaginable, literally blowing the users mind, throwing thoughts into a spin of magic, euphoria, adrenalin. A primal hunt for our desires and the kill that delivers, a positive memory, imprinting our brain with success, securing repetition.
3. When you don't deliver on an expectation, the users experience is shattered, creating a state of remorse. The user falls into discomfort, trying to processes and hold on to the desire there was, going through the stages of disbelief, denial, anger and finally acceptance, making the experience a negative memory, avoiding such cases in the future. Norepinephrine and epinephrine surge through the body fro

our adrenal system, getting ready for a fight-or-flight response, cooping with the experience. The customer is entering buyers remorse.

There is a force, a mentality, a culture, a way of life, ruling and shaping your design and its environment, I call it the *evolutionary force*.

This force is responsible for which technologies is springing to life, how modern branding works, best practice designs and how we interact with the digital world.

Understanding the evolutionary force of our time, will guide you to the true user experience. Like evolutionary attributes, the exceeding variations will progress to the next generation. The failing variations will die out and the variations that doesn't serve a purpose will be subject to random events.

The journey will imprint our brain with positive, negative and redundancy. It will guide us through what to pursue, what to avoid and what to trust. Our hunt for the better, the serene, the sweeter, the stronger is a primal survival instinct to be alive, to live, to be.

All great storytelling follows this process, taking you on a roller coaster ride, building desire and delivering relief. Each cognitive communication element will be observed as part of the journey and expected to deliver.

In motion design, gestures are an engaging journey, with expectations for each finger touching and interacting with the interface. By each press, there is an expectation of feedback. How you return this feedback will fall into the three levels of delivery. The user will assume that the hard surface will react as a minimum, mimicking the laws of physics. When we go beyond, enforcing the motion, the expectation will be exceeded and our brain is amazed, activating dopamine. When the motion is lacking behind, stuttering or feels stiff in contrast to the environment, the experience becomes a disappointment, activating anger.

No amount of marketing will make up for a bad product journey. Great products will sell them self, where good products are often wrapped in great marketing. This gab between the marketing campaign and the product standard, will create a tension of expectations if they do not align. If you oversell and create exciting slogans or campaigns, that raises my expectations towards an assumed great product, which then fails to deliver, the flaws becomes more than obvious, they become a statement of inferior design.

I've had my fair share of great marketing designs, selling inferior products, thus learning by bitter experience to keep a customers expectations aligned with the products.

Working with Microsoft® on their job campaigns, I studied the entire employee and employer journey, from when a candidate viewed the initial marketing posters, applied for the job, the feedback and resulting job interview. As Microsoft® had an employee philosophy to value the entire journey, putting high focus on job security and passion, we needed to align that philosophy with the actual journey and campaign. This resulted in a great campaign, while raising the entire journey to the same level. As we started to focus on the philosophy and the campaign we wanted to do, we started to see the flaws in the journey, which then raised the standard.

It's common to see a designers real intensions, expressed in marketing, as this is often an easy outlet for what isn't possible within a divided organization. A different scenario, is that the marketing campaign is created by an agency who had little or no insight into the why and how of the product, they are trying to sell.

If marketing is just added as circumstance of the product, it will never be able to connect with the customers and the product. Marketing has to be part of the product design, as this is where the initial journey are starting, followed by the product itself. The careful thoughts and extensive work implemented into the product, can't be lost or rethought when reaching the marketing department, as they have to be true to the story, following the journey.

SECTION 4

EXPRESSION

An experience is a cognitive overload, forcing us to focus and rewording us with excitement driven by dopamine as we pursue the enjoyment through time. When an experience present itself, we either pass it by as we are unaware of the impact or we chase it down as we are teased by the possibility and expectations of the dopamine high.

People don't enjoy products, they experience them, they inhale the satisfaction of being part of the brilliance and beauty that the designer have put time and effort into. It's a drug, an adrenalin rush when you get the true experience of a well crafted product which yells simplicity, domestication, beauty, function and magic. It's a fascination, a concept satisfaction, a true product indulgence.

As I walked down the street, a familiar face stood out in the crowd. He was walking towards me, as we started to gain eye contact. I couldn't remember where I knew him from, but his face was very familiar. It felt like we might have been colleagues or acquaintances some time ago. As he came close, I greeted him with an awkward sentence, "I know you from somewhere?". He was I bit confused, as he didn't seem to recognize me. "Have we worked together?", I added. "No I don't think so", he said, almost eager to get going.

With a bit of trial and error, I realized, that I didn't know him, but he had been on the daily commute almost a decade ago. Though I don't know him, that daily commute imprinted his face, along with all the others, in my memory through the years. It felt like, we almost knew each other, because my mind had slowly added more and more meaning to the faces each morning.

An experience is the feelings I have towards the product and the feelings I want from the product, as it gradually imprints my mind. I belong to my products, and they belong to me. To loosen that deep unquestionable feeling, your product has to brake it, shatter my devoted love towards these products.

Experiences are often not pure in their values and statements, as they are tainted by the marketing channel. The retail store, web-shops, apps, devices or environments who are selling or rendering the experience.

In larger department stores, premium brands are located side by side, trying to establish a unique in-store experience within their allocated square meters. The customer is influenced by the department store, the adjacent brands and the in-store experience, buying the product. Here, competition is fears, as the better offer might be next door. The neighboring shop, the staff and the first impressions, are vital to establishing a powerful emotional relation with the customer, even returning customers. The brands are part of a quickly evolving ecosystem, where you must evolve with your environment to sustain your products, adapting to your channels, competitors and resources.

In my spare time I enjoy seeing the sceneries of my city by bike, to a degree where I participate in triathlons and cross-country competitions. This is a summer sport, as the delicate mechanics and slim wheels of a carbon bike, is too fragile for the winter conditions. In the winter, my bike is parked in a home trainer, a device that transform the bike into a convenient spinning machine, a home training experience, without going anywhere.

The home trainer is based on a stand, to rest the rear of the bike and a flywheel. A flywheel is a heavy aluminum disc, that through repeated motion on the bike, can be spun into rotation. As you pedal, the flywheel starts to turn, picking up speed and momentum. The more momentum the flywheel gain, the more it can sustain the speed on its own, for a certain amount of time. It's hard to get started, but ones you reach an optimal speed, the flywheel will help you stay in momentum.

Customers emotional bond follows the same principles, as a strong and historical bond, will make op for occasional hiccups. If your brand has momentum with your customers, you can afford the unavoidable and occasional mistakes that will fall in your path. But like the flywheel analogy and the triathlon training, you have to keep pedaling, becoming stronger, faster and more agile.

Working at Bang & Olufsen, the luxury brand in audio and video products, is an exceptional strong emotional process of story telling, resonating with the market segment. Each story I told, would have to result in the magic that is Bang & Olufsen, creating luxurious moments in sound and display. Even though some products fail to hit the mark, the emotional relationship towards the brand and the products, are far greater than any hiccups along the way. Bang & Olufsen customers decorate their homes with design poetry, shaped like speakers and televisions, enjoying the pleasure of the emotional feedback the industrial and digital design is offering. Their loyalty is among the highest in the world, as some customers are reaching multiple decades of devotion.

CREATING AND CREATED EXPERIENCES, A DIVIDED MIND

Designing customer experiences, is an ability to play more than one instrument. Many designers have one angle of approach in common fields like prototyping, conceptualizing, user experience (UX), user interaction (UI), information architecture (IA) or art direction (AD). In the field of holistic customer experiences (CX) and service design, the primary task is the ability to understand the music, not the instruments. This ability is achieved by playing multiple instruments, as we start to understand the contrast between different tunes. When we understand the contrast, we start to understand the tunes and then the music. This big picture ability, give us the insight to our customers experiences, as they too are interested in the music, not the instrument.

A product experience is divided into the creating and created experience, a divided mind between enjoying the act of creating a product or enjoying using a product.

When we focus on the instrument, we are in a *creating experience zone*. When we focus on the music, we are in a *created experience zone* or what designers call the customer moment. Because of this, we often loose focus on the customer, if we only focus on the instrument and creating the experience.

This dilemma is in all areas of passionated work, like writing a book. Writing and reading are synonyms for the two mindsets. When you write, you enjoy creating experiences, when you read, you enjoy the created experiences.

When I write, I enjoy creating an experience for my readers, typing each word and processing my thoughts into keyboard strokes. But that experience is mine, and it is not intended for my readers. It is a hobby, something I do in my spare time with a cup of coffee while relaxing in my chair surrounded by music. That experience is completely different from the end result, the created experience, that I will soon enjoy when i proofread my book. In that process, I often find mistakes or problems with the flow of words, simply because I add a different mindset to the experience. In this process, it is no longer about enjoying creating phrases, but instead enjoying the created phrases.

If we focus on the details within the process of en experience, we loose sight of the process and the result. Playing one instrument will force you to focus on a single tune, as you don't have the ability to understand the symphony. If we understand all the instruments, we understand the symphony and the customer within it, giving us the ability to both enjoy creating the experience and the created experience.

TO BELIEVE IN A PRODUCT, WE MUST EXPERIENCE IT

Trust and believe is a relationship between knowledge and emotions. I define knowledge as logical information which could be true or false, regardless of what we understand to be true or false. I define emotions as a psychological respond or addictive behavior, an illogical force within. We reach trust and believe when all knowledge or feelings points in one strong direction.

Basically, humans understand very little on all subjects and we fill in the blanks with believe, derived from our emotional relationship with the subject. Our emotional respond to objects and living things, creates a flight or respond reaction, a cognitive behavior that we use to believe in what we don't fully understand. You start to believe, when your emotions reach a deeper cognitive connection. Your emotional bond can be broken by logic, achieved by knowledge, a trust that can overcome your own feelings.

Think of any relationship in your life; how well do you truly know this person, how often had you argued over the same things or the same feelings? In your mind, you might be kindred spirits, though you don't fully understand each other, but your combined emotional relationship creates a deep believe in each other, thus you believe in your relationship.

Thinking of my own relationship with my father and mother, I will never fully understand them, but a lifetime of knowledge and emotional bonds, has created a trust and believe that seams unbreakable.

My best friends through decades are often arguing over the same mundane topics, things they by know should be aligned on, but aren't, simply because they will never fully understand these dividing subjects.

Your might think you understand everything there is to know on a subject, merely because you believe you know everything. You believe in the emotions that surround your partial understanding, leading you to proclaim or reject any subject. As your knowledge grows, so will the tipping point of your trust. In equal measures, emotion will always win over knowledge, as it is tied to a cognitive perception, covering more receptors in our brain.

When products, services or relationships fails to resonate, it can be credited to mistrust or disbelieve. A great product design balance emotions and knowledge towards the customer, as emotions offers loyalty and knowledge offers credibility.

The anti tobacco industry has been fighting with knowledge against emotions, for ages. Even though a box of cigarettes are labeled with horrifying images of cancer, skeleton illustrations or clear warnings, the emotional tie, the addiction, is far greater than any knowledge will ever be, as emotions can reach a deeper level. Thus, you will never be smart enough to overcome your addiction. To win this battle, they need to battle on the same domain, a fight with emotions against emotions.

The same logic applies to over eaters. Most people know that pizzas, burgers and greasy fast food in general, is unhealthy, but we still pursue the quick and easy meal options. We are emotional bond to the addictions, the sugar satisfaction, the moment and excitement. If I want to loose weight and overcome my over eating behavior, I have to either gain enough knowledge to logically deny myself these guilty pleasures or tie an even stronger emotional bond with a healthy ideology, creating a breakup with my previous emotions.

While giant established organizations are fighting for mass market shares, through quantitative product features, the disruptors are achieving loyal shares through feature quality, creating emotional and relatable products.

Looking at the battle between PlayStation and xBox, each generation is improved with more memory, more speed and more features, with very little attention to design or the emotional relation towards the device or the platform. They fight over the amount of customers they can force through their array of products, services and accessories, calculating each sale as a unique entity. This battle has a simple outcome; the organization who can sustain the longest and with the most amount of revenue, will win. The problem with this battle is that anyone can participate, as each organization is working on a duplicatable model of success.

The Android and iPhone debate is also intriguing, as most people relate brand against brand, debating over what product delivers the best range of features. But the debate has nothing today with what Apple or Google is offering their customers, as they don't compete directly against each other. The Android platform is pursuing mass market shares and Apple is pursuing loyal market shares. They are working with two different models, with different goals. While you could duplicate and challenge the Google model, which is build on a tangible business strategy, you can't duplicate the Apple model, which is build on a strategy submerged in their customers emotional devotion. Achieving an Apple model will require gaining loyalty and devotion from emotional invested customers.

I hear this often, “why don’t we just do what apple is doing?”. Because we can’t duplicate their model and hence their success, we can’t just do what Apple is doing or any other company who have achieved loyal market shares. To build this loyalty, you must establish your brand, your products and thereby gain a customer believe in your company.

Coca-Cola® is the second most known word in the world, only surpassed by word hello. The word is unmistakably connected to the sugary beverage of the same name, a brand that has an immense emotional impact and trust among their loyal customers. Though Coca-Cola® is catering for the mass market, they sustain their position by relating to their customers, who believe in the product.

Other words like jacuzzi, thermos or walkman, are not words either, but brands that has lost their connection with their products, as they have become the term to describe a category of products by the entire industry. I often hear the word jeep being used to define a recreational vehicle, not in the context of the brand Jeep®. This happens when knowledge is disconnected from believe, as knowledge can be associated with any product and used in any business model.

The ability to apply a customers believe to another product, is impossible as emotions are tied to the cognitive experience and memory. The trust however is an illusion based on perceived facts, that can just as easily be true for other products. We can move our trust, when the invested logic apply to the competition and we feel comfortable switching to the better offer. But we can't move our believe, as it will require an emotional bond or breakup, which takes time to establish.

While driving down the west-coast of Oregon, I had a sleepover at the Old Town motel in Florence. This quint little town, with its sand dunes and almost southern lakes and beautiful crossing bridges, gave me my first experience at the water front, in what seemed like a designed experience. Despite the help of both Google and Trip Advisor, me and my wife stumbled over a very little restaurant placed at the food of the lake, the Waterfront Depot. As we came through the door of what looked like the kitchen entrance, the waiter greeted us with a welcoming smile, like she had expected us for many days. Though no table was available, we where guided into a small cozy gazebo where we could enjoy a drink while waiting, with an extraordinary scenic view over the glittering water, reflecting the moon. As we got seated, the night turned into a magical experience, with small gastronomic plates of delicious creations, that suited our gourmet critical tastebuds. As we where savoring the last drops of wine and crumbs of our desserts, we looked over the small restaurant floor, seating the local community in lively laughter. The wooden decor and the dimmed lighting gave us an almost intimate cabin experience. A comfortable and delightful night that will linger in my mind for decades. When I return to Florence, I'll have a burning desire to return to this experience, relive those feelings and once again savor the moments.

Though the price might be higher than an average McDonald's, the experience has created an emotional bond that will be part of my restaurant choices and expectations forever. This foodie story is not unique and we can all rekindle such a moment, as we have bonded with a specific setting and circumstance. Though McDonald's is catering for the mass market, I am not immune to their offers, even when I feel that I have to compromise by choosing a Big Mac, their food fits certain circumstances of mine, when time, price and location is a factor in a quick and easy meal choice. But even though I can fall to temptation for the McDonald's offers, I can't remember a single McDonald's moment, as there is nothing magical about this compromise, because it is a compromise. Their products doesn't fall above or below my expectations.

McDonald's cater for the mass market, thus catering for the lowest denominator. As I want more than the lowest denominator, I will always want more than McDonald's can offer. Because of this, the McDonald's brand only serve as my fast food chain of choice, while it holds no emotional value, it does stand as the standard within their market tier. As the brand holds no emotional value, it won't hold any feelings towards their existence, as removing McDonald's from my list of choices, would only pull the next fast food chain on the list, to the top. If the Waterfront Depot would be gone at my next road trip, even years from now, I would feel the equivalent of a small heartbreak, having to let go of the emotions, the memories and expectations that was in store and attached to that place in time.

Could such a restaurant be designed into a mass market chain or would such an experience only serve as the unique experience it was for me and my wife. As the mass market is a numbers game, the numbers will always win over the magic that creates the emotional bonding moments. The key is to refine each restaurant and outlet with as much adjustability as possible, creating a concept that fits the staff, the price tier and the circumstances that drives business by the window. While acclaimed chefs opens restaurant after restaurant, this move could be seen as individual restaurants, a desired perception, as the reality is the creation of a chain in the name of a renowned chef, a gourmet designer. While the concept looks different on the outside and through the menu, it is simply yet another product by the same designer.

While mass market product design seams impossible to capture emotions, as the amount of user relations you would have to capture, is an extensive algorithm, it is not impossible. Mass market design is the ability to capture millions or billions of peoples feelings, falling in love with your products. The experience of such products are nearly impossible, but by playing on the most primitive feelings, shared by all humans, you can achieve such devotion.

In the sports industry, the emotions run through the masses when a beloved team win or loses, as seen by mass hysteria and celebrations in the streets. Sport is an emotional topic for many people when talking about specific teams, competing against each other. The very nature of competitions or game mentality, is an addictive and thus emotional attachment to the act of gaming or competing. The believe in a team is also an emotional need to be part of a group combined with the adrenaline of sport.

In the movie industry, emotions are captured by the masses in an often vivid experience, through the big screen. The product, in this case a movie, can offer an incredible story telling, incorporating adventure, horror, comedy, action or romance, bonding by a visual and audible cognitive experience in a social setting.

While your product might not be a game or a movie, it is important to understand where the emotions are attached, as your focus is on the product. In games and movies, emotions are often attached to characters portraying a role, while the producers or directors are often forgotten, thereby rendering the product mute by its own content. This is often the case with TV products, as the TV itself becomes unimportant in relation to the amount of content within, reducing the product to a simple screen on the wall, which can quickly be replaced by any screen by any brand. For the TV to play a role in the emotional context, it needs to be part of the story, the function, the journey and the experience.

Studies have shown that people favor quantity over quality, when they don't trust or believe in the subtleties of the product. When people don't see the added value in acquiring quality, quantity becomes the favored commodity, as this is an easy measurement. To promote quality, people need to resonate and understand the added value, thus favoring the quality over quantity. In design, when quality is a principle, your customers must understand the added value, as it must serve a purpose. To define the purpose, quality must be embedded in your story, your function, your journey and the final product experience.

At 801 Mission St., in San Francisco, one of Mel's drive-in diners will take you back in time, with a retro look and a wide selection of comfort food. There is nothing special nor extraordinary about their food, but sometimes, it is just what you need. At the menu, you will find grass-fed meat and organic produce, raising your expectations in the food your tastebuds are about to enjoy.

I ordered a mushroom burger and a strawberry shake, as this is my typical feel-good combo. The burger was at the expected standard, neither raising nor lowering my experience in what I expected to get from my already raised expectations. But the shake came with a surprise, an additional bowl of ice cream, leftovers from the blend. As I was not custom to this offering, I was surprised to get an additional shake, simply because there was more from the blend, than what could fit in the glass. I starred at the additional bowl of blended ice cream and the glass of strawberry shake with the sherry on top.

As I enjoyed this delicious surprise, an ice cream moment, I now embarked on a new experience, one that will raise the level of expectations for milk shakes, an extra bowl of leftovers when I needed to indulge myself. I will now always compare my shakes to Mel's as long as they hold the standard compared to the expectations I have, relative to the price and circumstance.

A week later, I landed on the small island of Bornholm, an island known for its danish gourmet experiences and sceneries. In the town square of Svaneke, the locals produce fresh licorice, chocolate, ice cream, caramel, pasta, mustard and beer. Micro vendors and distilleries, a combination of factory and boutique in each shop, a tourist attraction, using local and organic ingredients. The milk was almost warm, as it came from cows at the adjacent farms. The chocolate had a rich dark flavor, made from centuries of tradition. The licorice had a spicy attitude, inspired by the neighborhood culture. This town square felt as it was designed to be a gourmet hub. The design principles all came together right here.

I walked into the ice cream shop and ordered a strawberry shake. The waitress opened a canister of freshly made strawberry ice cream, made that morning, including only hole milk into the blender. She knew exactly how much ice cream and milk was needed, as the result was a perfect match to the cup she handed me, as she gave me a straw and a smile. I walked outside, sat down in the sun, enjoyed the view over the flea market and the people around me, as I got the first taste of my strawberry shake. The taste was almost unique and I wouldn't compare it to anything I have tasted before, it was a league on it s own. This shake was an unexplainable experience, as I felt a rich taste of strawberry and milk unknown to my senses, a luxurious ice cream moment was born.

When customers know the market to be good-enough, they crave quantity. Then more is better, as the good-enough is better in large quantities.

When customers know the market to be below their expectations, they crave quality. Then less is better, as the quality alone, will continuously surprise the expected satisfaction.

A moment is the first drag of a cigaret, the luxurious moment is enjoying the entire cuban cigar.

A moment is the first sip of an ice-cold cola, the luxurious moment is swirling a glass of chilled whisky on the rocks.

A moment is the exaggerated milkshake from Mel's, the luxurious moment is slurp of a Svaneke organic milkshake by the harbor.

You might not enjoy either of these luxurious moments and that is exactly the point. The luxurious moment is about knowing the nuances and intricate subtleties. If we don't understand its complexity, we don't appreciate its beauty.

This is as valid from a customer point of view, as it is from a designers point of view. Your customers, clients or colleagues might not see the same beauty as you, simply because they don't appreciate or perceive the complexity in your work. That doesn't mean that it isn't a moment and your work isn't valid, but it might not be as luxurious as you perceive it to be or give it the ability to be. If our customers can't get to the same understanding as you, then they will never perceive the same experience as you.

CHAPTER 4

MANAGE

"Design is cultivating your principles, your deliverables, your learnings."

Managing design is an art form, a beautiful orchestrated cultivation of your product and corporate principles, shaping the deliverables of inputs and outputs, by defining the responsibilities and deadlines of each deliverable.

This chapter will define management as a nourishing and responsible culture, shaped by product principles and the deliverables needed to gain approval within a team, an organization or with your client. Managing design demands creative and adaptable leaders, working towards new opportunities, not defending the status quo.

The four principles of management will guide you through rules, processes, culture and deliverables, understanding your team and their learnings.

The principles of design management are,

1. **Insight**, gathering ideas and synthesizing learnings into the organization. Design must solve known customer problems, seamless from past learnings.
2. **Exploration**, sharing knowledge and establishing a mutual department launch pad. Design must have a platform for growth and agility throughout the organization.
3. **Relation**, defining a meaningful customer synergy, between loyal customers and social marketing channels. The entire value chain must have a common language, to express their shared believe.
4. **Solution**, a united and focused direction from current goals. Design must be aligned and uncompromised within the organization. Pick your battles, double down and spend time together. Through challenges and achievements, perception and management, allocating the required knowledge will make the product plausible.

The first two principles, *insight* and *exploration*, are your opening phases, defining your product, capturing the recipe for making your gourmet experience. As you approach the *relation* and *solution* phases, your product is well defined and documented, ready for production.

Getting the right management is crucial for achieving your results, as the wrong managers will fail to move your organization in the desired direction. Often management are hired or put in charge by their organizational or people skills, validated on their previous uninterrupted success. Design as a business, requires entrepreneuring managers who can innovate, work with abstract market solutions and continuously shifting trends. Because of this, they must be able to bring disruptions to the market and to the organization.

Having a long experience in large organizations with sustaining innovation, keeping the status quo, does not grant you the experience needed to adventure into disruptive innovations. Sustaining innovations requires a broad view on the market and the competitions, as disruptive innovation requires an in-depth knowledge on the breakthrough and emerging market, that your product will conquer. While I use the term product as physical, digital or service, the product could also be an internal restructure or transformation in the organization.

When you go through the four principles of management, these principles must be managed by people who have in-depth knowledge of these areas, leading by example while understanding their area of expertise. The manager or managers of each principle, must be at the frontier of their experience, setting the industry standard and adding to the shared knowledge in the organization and community, as they innovate products.

While the modern organizations are facing more complex and quick shifting markets, dealing with advanced customer designs, managers must be collaborative, communicative, creative and flexible. They should constantly focus on self development by reinventing themselves, learning as they go, as this mentality is attuned to the markets they pursue.

CULTIVATING YOUR TEAM

Culture is derived from an emotional relationship to your organizational processes and values, which is derived from unstructured resources, in desperate search of order. Design management, is the art of managing design, a company expression, a shared believe, a culture. Nurturing your design and the culture, will create a trust far greater than the product. Believing in people and their visions, through culture, can be unbreakable, as it becomes an ideology across multiple departments.

Culture is a powerful management tool for working with the organizational capabilities and disabilities of processes and people, who believe in the culture. This believe will strengthen your processes and values, as people will act autonomously and consistently within their believe, like a chemical pheromone, they will act on instincts. But the same positive nature will also make it hard to adjust the organization, as a culture is a heavy boulder to move when change is needed.

Management is not the most exciting word and many people have a toxic relationship with this term. My definition of management is to inspire and lead by cultivating principles, that will serve you when you hit the wall, ensuring coherent products throughout your portfolio.

There is difference between leading people and managing people in an organization. As a leader, you inspire the why, as a manager, you cultivate the how. It's not a question about choosing, but knowing the difference. As a designer you will need to do both, going through the process, improving your skills, your team and your products. Leadership is not something you can read about and theorize, it's experienced and embodied through hard work and practical learnings.

The ancient sketch depict the manager in a chariot, demanding his slaves into the work ahead, forcing his will upon them, while the leader is the slave who stand at the front, pulling the manager and his peers by sheer will power and determination. This sketch is far from the reality, though not unheard, the sketch do paint the distinction between the two roles.

As a leader, you inspire by your work, integrity, dedication and the ethics you follow, as an undomesticated designer, creating an ideology around you. You can emphasize with your team and relate to their perception, giving them the practical and theoretical insight or aspect they need.

As a manager, you implement work by solid ideas and principles, creating strategies and rules to be followed with the premise; make people understand and support the instructions, let them make it their own, let them take ownership and feel responsible, creating a working culture.

Supervising your team by merely evaluating their work without offering work of your own, instructing them to do better and work harder, is neither management nor leadership, its redundant and degrading, in the premise; your team should already live and breath such simple work ethics within a strong team culture. If this is not the case, then revisit your strategies and reboot your team, don't tell them what to do, show them what to do, while being ready to answer both the why and how of your process.

As a manager your job is to create a safe heaven for discovering challenges, not limiting risks, but making it safe to take them. As a leader your job is to inspire achievements, breaking with safe ground, finding the ultimate answers in the blue sky. Combining leadership and management, will create the knowledge of possibilities, with a culture of comfort and structure.

Design knowledge and ability within an organization, is only as strong as your executive level, e.g. your COO, Head of Design or Head of Product. This person is responsible for leading and recruiting senior designers and managers, who again is responsible for recruiting designers with various skills, e.g. UI, UX, graphic design and concept design. In this chain, each level must add more knowledge to the company, than the person managing, as the organization must keep adding to their shared knowledge, extending their abilities. If the senior or executive manager isn't capable of judging or assessing the ability to bring true design value and skills to the company, the recruited knowledge will taint the company, as work and ability will degraded the teams efforts. The senior managers must know what the true essence of design is, as they are responsible for continuously validating and polishing the work of their staff. Furthermore, the executive level is responsible for defining the overall company standard, ideology and culture on design, as it must be embedded as a business strategy.

High achieving designers don't work for the company, they work for the shared believe within the company, they work for the challenges and achievements, they work for them self and their peers, they work for the product.

As a designer, you need inspiration and motivation, following ideologies that thigh you to your work. Managing a design culture is about failing, sharing, learning and succeeding, creating an environment of open dialog and positive attitudes.

Designers sees them self a individuals, therefore the culture must embrace the individual. You might have a structured chain of commands, but the chain of information should be linear.

Relentless improvements and continuous knowledge is key to any success. As this is the driver, you need an organization, a team with the capacity to be lean and fast, moving as the insight dictates. As your improvements will reduce redundancies and optimize your cadence, knowledge will be your strength.

HIGH ACHIEVERS

I hire high achievers, self-made professionals, passionates who have learned from their scars. I don't want you to show me your diplomas or resumé. I want you to impress me, engage me and win my respect by your unquestionable self-believe and experience you have earned through your adventures spirit and life learnings.

I wan't your potential, I don't wan't your knowledge, as I don't know if that will help me, when markets are shifting and the product must follow. If you have the ability to learn new skills when required, you have the ability to design your way through disruptive products and the always changing production process. If we only hire what is need, our managers and designers becomes a simple fix to a current problem. We must hire for the future and their ability to adapt to that future. We must value their potential more than their current set of skills. If they can acquire skills when need, then that is their true skill.

There is a misconception in our industry, that a persons ability to perform in an unknown field by management, is also capable of performing on any level in that field. Just because your nephew know how to create a website, doesn't make him capable of operating your core digital strategy, like my brother in-law isn't capable of creating skyscrapers just because he is a gifted craftsman or a drug addict can perform open heart surgery, simple because he know how to operate a syringe.

The tip-of-the-iceberg ability are often interpreted as the ability to fix an enterprise problem, simply because management can't see the iceberg below water. As they can't see it, the ability match the problem from their perspective.

This is often seen, when fresh out of collage students or inexperienced designers become responsible for enterprise decisions, unaware of the delicate processes and underlaying knowledge needed to perform successful in these scenarios.

The lack of knowledge, is the number one problem in any industry, from executive management to production. We must all know and grasp the size of our achievement, as our knowledge must be equal to the job at hand. If we lack the knowledge, we must pursue and challenge our way true new learnings before we can achieve, acquiring new skills.

A team must consist of different stages of expertise, ranging from trainees to seniors. Cultivating a career path through these stages, is crucial to the teams shared knowledge and expertise.

The shared knowledge of your team is based on every element that will enforce your decision making process, man or machine.

Each stage brings its own level of expertise, personal motivation and approach to product development. Picking the right combination will ensure a healthy working symbiosis.

You need the four primary minds of design, a poet, an engineer, an architect and an artist, with a balanced degree of expertise.

On-boarding new designers is important to make them get acquainted with the people and their shared believes, inject them into the culture, make them feel welcome and part of the traditions, the principles and the dialog. If you feel a sense of disorganization and disharmony within the teams, like fractured believes and understandings, you start to feel discomfort, as the organization is not aligned. You will notice that people are uninformed and unknowing of the company trajectory and strategy.

This feeling is the poison that will slowly kill any inspiration, engagement and happiness within the workplace, as people fall into a confined role, just doing the job. Left behind is the possibilities, the excitement and the extra effort that could have made the difference.

Creating career opportunities and the ability to advance, is important for a designer to spread his or her wings, evolving on a personal level, moving the company along in the process.

Career levels,

1. **Trainee**, is the inexperienced and finds even the most mundane elements of the design process, new and exciting. He or she is the spirit of the team. He or she would be unaware of the tools to solve the simplest problems and doesn't have the knowledge to find them. You would not be able to estimate his deliveries or the quality thereof, neither would he or she. When a problem blocks his path, he or she would not be able to solve it, thereby failing to progress. He or she need constant supervision and a skilled teacher to guide him or her through obstacles.
2. **Junior**, has preferably 3 years practical experience, not counting studying. He or she is the daredevil of the team, the first platoon, because he or she dons't know the consequences. He or she would be unaware of the tools to solve general problems, the easy wins, but has the knowledge to find them with time. He or she would be able to estimate a delivery, but not the quality thereof and neither would he or she, even though he or she differ on that opinion, slowly growing his or hers own ego. He or she would be unable to predict problems in his path, but can recover and continue

with delay. He or she need a skilled mentor and a good colleague to share his or hers ideas with.

3. **Senior**, has preferably 6-9 years practical experience. He or she can predict the problems ahead, prepare himself for the impact and recover quickly as he or she moves in a new direction, securing and solving the issue as a simple routine. As a senior designer, you have responsibilities to your team, inspire and share with them, as you learn by traveling your own path.
4. **Lead**, has preferably 9-12 years practical experience. He or she is the teacher of the team, the second wave. He or she can predict the problems ahead for the entire team, prepare for the impact and recover quickly as he or she moves the team in a new direction. As a lead designer, you have responsibilities for managing your team, lead them and inspire them by creativity, vision and ingenuity.

NO GAIN, NO PAY!

How confidence are you in your designs and your theories? In recent years, I started to get bored of my design work, as I was missing the thrills of the challenges. On the same note, I had submerged my designs in business logic and strategies, in order to gain the best possible outcome of my creations. That led me to *no gain, no pay*.

If my clients didn't gain any value from my creations, neither should I. On each new project with a new client, we started by stating the business goals and my KPI in that context. If I reached a KPI tier, I would get paid on that tier, if I didn't, I would have learned a valuable lessen, trusting my pay check with my strategies and tactics.

As a business and design consultant, advising entrepreneuring startups and established enterprises, I must admit that I did learn a couple of valuable lessens, but through these learnings I gained some incredible insights because of the stakes I added. If there where no consequence to my work, I might not have had the personal drive to research the root cause of those failures, finding valuable insights that will forever propel my projects.

In any type of work, it's important to added an incentive to learn from both success and failures. If you neglect to dive into your failures from sheer shame or simply cast a blind eye to their existence, you will never be able to overcome your own abilities and further your projects. You're better than that. If you neglect to understand the underlaying metrics to your successes, you will never see what you did to actually achieve success. In any case, be willing to understand the real success and failure in your designs.

SECTION 1

INSIGHT

Ideation, sharing ideas and inspiring your colleagues. Design must solve known customer problems, seamless from past learnings.

Ideas are easy, everyone can and will get a bright idea, but being able to follow your ideas from theory to practical application, is the job of the design team. Work out the metrics, the structure and the experience of your ideas, so that they become actual plans, not just ideas, but plans you can implement and set in efficient motion.

There is a goal here, a message to be conveyed through this process. Your are communicating through each stage, shaping your product one layer at the time, starting at the core.

Gathering resources and inspiration outside your team, is vital to evolving your shared knowledge. If you only rely on your engineers, architects and designer within your team, combined with your own knowledge, your shared knowledge will become static and over time degrade in quality, resulting in blind productions, unaware of the world outside.

Using external consultants, innovations and technologies will give you a leap towards your products goals and influence you with new cultural norms and teachings. When you introduce a foreign element to your team, as with new technologies, the culture within the team will either accept it or reject it. The new element is coated in the culture of its producer and you can embrace and learn from that.

External influences, processes and tools are often rejected by the people who server the existing culture, seeing the foreign elements as an infection, introduced to their natural ecosystem. Like white blood cells, the employees reject and fight the foreign elements, which they don't recognize as their own. To implement foreign elements to your ecosystem, you must understand the ecosystem and the placement of the element, as your culture must see the element as their own, by its natural order in the culture.

Every time I walk into a meeting, I remind myself that; on the other side of the door, are people waiting with expectations. No matter what type of meeting or what side of the table you are seated at, there is a hidden agenda within all participants. Their agenda will be different from yours, even worse, their perspective for each item on their mental checklist, will be different from yours. Their expectations will be on all levels; inputs, outputs and social validation, to be heard, to be understood and to be present.

Every time I remind my self to perceive their agenda, using my experience to guide and nurture their presence, aligning them with mine. It's not manipulation, but validating their thoughts against yours, succeeding in giving them gratification and solving their mental checklist, which often precede the practicalities of the meeting.

Meetings is a social gathering of the design team, aligning and adding order, maintaining the status and evolving the relationship. Each meeting will have to succeed the previous, nurturing the relationship and establishing a further bond. As your participation becomes stronger and more reliable, your presence will be more acceptable, adding value to the team. A team must know what each member is bringing to the table, the knowledge they each offer, thus changing the assumption of knowledge to actual abilities and influence, clearly defining their roles and tasks.

While the practical outcome of the meeting is important and usual the basis for the meeting, the social context and bonding will supersede in value, as this will create validation and resonation in your design process. Networking your designs, is the key to getting support and traction with your team, clients and organization, being relatable as a design manager.

Years of experience, previous success and glory as a designer, is not relatable. I don't believe in subjectivity, I don't believe in what I can't see, I don't believe in what I can't understand. I believe in personal relations, I believe in you, I believe in your action, I believe in your principles. Don't tell me what you know, show me what you know.

You can't just flash a career resumé against a client or a colleague, thinking that your previous success is the validation you need to define your position and secure your agenda, establishing your throne from where your words will resonate like the ten commandments. You need to be liked, to be accepted as the person you are, not the person you wish to be.

Brainstorming and brainwriting are popular used practices, when tackling new market opportunities, by reaching consensus amongst your team. While brainstorming is a social game that often favor those who speak up, brainwriting is a more equal practice for the introverts and extroverts. Through brainwriting, you add your thoughts to a piece of paper, quickly adding them to a pool of ideas, while you pass them to your colleagues on your left, who add to the specific idea. As the pool reaches a desired amount, a pattern will start to emerge by categorizing the ideas into concept groups. In teams of minimum five people, this game often results in breaking the first ground on new frontiers.

While leading a brainwriting session, save the ideas that do emerge, as people have a tendency to feel overlooked or unappreciated. Every idea has to be grouped and added to an idea bank for future reference, adding to the bank with each brainwriting session. As these sessions must be used as a continuous practice, each session must be either started or spun-off as a summery of the previous ideas, thereby elaborating and updating the banks value.

WOVEN KNOWLEDGE

The idea is a powerful perception, as it is so strong to our mental state, born from thoughts through thousand of hours. Your specific idea might be a spur of the moment, as it explodes into your conscious, but it is building upon many thoughts and ideas through your career. To bring an idea to live, you must go through many threads of thought, as you weave your epiphany. To share such an idea with others, can be an almost impossible task, as they haven't gone through the same thought process as you, and to bring it forth, you must reconstruct your process for them.

I can't count how many time I have stated, what is an obvious observation for me, but an almost inconceivable construct for my colleagues. As we are discussing the merits of design, we sometimes fall into the dilemma of woven knowledge.

The instinct you think you have, is the knowledge that you base your thoughts and discussions upon. When ever you must decide on a solution, your thoughts will guide you in one specific direction. These thoughts are the result of many previous conclusions, building on each other, as you pass through your career. These threads form in our unconscious mind, establishing your perceived instincts.

When we experience conflicts on ideas with our colleagues or clients, these instincts can quickly become a problem, as they often can't be explained. Your instincts is an unconscious basis for decisions, often woven into your memory as how, not why. You know what is true, you know how to solve the puzzle, but you can't explain why. The dilemma doubles, when your colleagues have the same instincts, though from a different perspective, threaded into a different solution. In such circumstances, your ideas won't align as they are competing against each other, woven from different perspectives into different solutions. Even when your knowledge is build on scientific theories and facts, your colleague won't know why you came to your conclusions, as he or she is still bond to their perceived fact.

To solve the conflict, it's important to take a step back, look at the solutions, reconstruct the thought process and learn the why. Your colleagues might not do the same and to find the right solution, you must include them in the process as they must be part of the result. Unthread these different perspectives and reconstruct them as one, as you will interpret a new shared and common ground.

These conflicts is the most common type of problem between colleagues, as they all think they have the answer, even though they only believe to know the solution. When we enter such conflicts, we quickly forget each others threaded length and will always add more value to our own instinct, as we believe it to be right, since it's woven into our knowledge.

I know why you shouldn't use competing bold labels, as the styling act as an attention seeker, thus confusing the user who can't focus. Because I know why, I also know how to explain and teach the perfect font weight, as I have gained this ability from research and scientific studies, understanding the users mental model.

I know how to design the perfect icon, but I don't know why, as I have learned this ability through woven knowledge. Many failed and succeeded results have filtered the bad from the good. I can't teach this ability, as I don't know the science behind it, the users mental process. This often results in a dilemma, when a colleague disagree, rendering decades of knowledge useless in a simple phrase. As I can't explain it, they can't understand it, thus competing for the assumption to be right.

Knowledge must be rooted in scientific exploration, as it must be taught. For knowledge to become knowledge, we must learn. It's important to accept the advanced and demanding process of achieving design and that each achievement will only get more demanding. That the gifted idea, might not be possible because of the exponential requirements.

SECTION 2

EXPLORATION

Sharing knowledge and establishing a mutual department launch pad, is important for creating a faster internal exploration, evolving the innovation and strength of the organization. Design must have a platform for growth and lean agility, throughout the departments.

Your design team is the most important component of the design process and without a coherent team, who can follow your examples, your team and your platform won't evolve, moving the departments along.

Picking the right people and creating the right culture around them, will create the necessary conditions for an efficient production flow.

Teaching within your team, is an easy way to grow your shared knowledge and in the process, strengthening the knowledge of the teacher by his or her own words.

As an example, an engineer must know why 11 + 11 = 22. We all know it's 22, even children, but why is it 22, is the question a teacher must ask, even in the process of teaching. Otherwise the believe and therein the quality of the knowledge is fragile and neither the student nor the teacher will learn fully from this relationship.

Senior developers has an extensive knowledge, but some of these bits of knowledge might be based on the how and not the why. Teaching and cultivating sharing, within your team, will fill these bits of knowledge.

When bits of information is brought to its fullest, edges is defined and can be crossed, bridges can form between bits and they becomes blocks of enlightenment and epiphanies.

The math behind the question, why is 11 + 11 = 22, is relative to the numeric base value. 11 + 11 = 22, because we use decimal numbers as a standard in modern society, also known as base ten numbers. If we where using binary numbers, also known as base two numbers, 11 + 11 = 110. The recursive value of each numeric index, is multiplied by its base and equal to the incremental sum.

While teaching a designer at Disney®, I was often given a question in return for my instruction, as every step was important to my student. While I was focusing on the how in each of my instructions, she was more interested in the why, as this would validate the how. This eager perception of her, gave the instructions more merit as each had to be theorized before practiced.

REMOVING REDUNDANCY

Working at Lycos®, together with Jubii® and Spray®, my first task was to change advertisement production and the surrounding systems as a system architect. When analyzing the workflow and customer situations, I learned that every detail was done by hand. When a customer wanted to run an ad campaign, they would ship the advertisement to Lycos®, who would then channel the communication to a traffic department, responsible for the campaign segments. The traffic department would use on-staff graphic designers, to validate and comment on the campaign within 24 hours, before going live on the affiliate networks.

After understanding the behavior of this workflow, I started working on a system that would replace any human relation in the validation and support of the advertisement. With the new designed platform in place, the customers advertisement, would go directly from accounting to the system by simply forwarding the customers initial email, which then analyzed the possible defects or errors in the campaign attachments, resulting in a to-the-point explanation, in such details that the customer or agency had no problem towards correcting the issue.

As the system wasn't hindered by any amount of work to be done, it could create best-practice explanation on popular topics for great campaigns within seconds, correcting errors and teaching the customer in the process. You might think that a system couldn't possibly replace the intuition and service level offered by humans, but as the system wasn't constrained by any workload and prioritization, the system could create the best known communication, going into details on the discovered errors in the attachments. As a result of this, the customer satisfaction increased and the feedback time was reduced by 80%. This created a greater turnaround throughout the channel of communication and an overall quicker customer dialog.

Within the company, the system liberated resources which could now focus on greater customer care, establishing a better footing on the market by removing meaningless redundancy. Removing redundancy is an important discipline to streamline you work and focus your resources on what is important.

The repetitive category of tasks, compared to the repetitive workflow of tasks. There are two schools of thoughts on the repetition of tasks, dividing the industry, either by completing each workflow and the individual tasks within, or by completing each category and the multiple tasks within. By completing each category of tasks, before moving on to the next, would suggest that you quickly learn the specific tasks, increasing in speed, routine and perfection of that specific type of task. In contrast, by completing each workflow and the different tasks within, would suggest that you spend to much time on reacquiring the routine in each individual task in the repetitive workflow. Though the two approaches are very different, there is no right or wrong choice between them.

The category approach is the fastest, but requires a larger commitment and offers where little room for adjustment, thus being highly lucrative by betting on success. This practice is often perceived as the best, but as the problems can quickly become multiplied by the very nature of the practice, the practice must be operated by careful and skilled precision. Each failure in this practice will destroy the entire production batch.

The workflow approach is the most adaptable and reliable, but requires an iterative commitment that will be more time consuming if overhead isn't removed. By completing each workflow by its single tasks, you can adjust by each iteration of the workflow, thereby adjusting by the learnings of each iteration. As this practice offers a more reliable and changeable process, the work can be operated with little skill, as failure wont destroy an entire production batch, but only the single workflow.

One afternoon I got peckish for an apple pie and opened the fridge, grabbing a dozen apples. The recipe was quite simple, wash, slice and boil the apples.

I washed the apples one by one and sliced them all one by one. When I started to boil the apples, I started to notice that the picture in the recipe didn't resemble my result, as the picture didn't have skin on the apple slices.

I forgot to peal the apples, but that mistake ruined a dozen apples, as I had to redo the recipe.

If I instead had washed, sliced and boiled each apple one by one, I would have noticed the mistake with the first apple, saving the rest of the batch.

This anecdote might be an easy mistake to fix, but imagine if we where talking mainstream production with millions of products and tasks, how much would you be ready to loose on assumptions and possible mistakes along the production flow. If you're not certain about the outcome, minimize the production batch.

SECTION 3

RELATION

Imagine a house, an elegant house with a beautiful garden, small uniquely selected flower arrangements, luxuriously parked car, all fitting together perfectly, on the outside. This house is stunning, the neighbors envy the thought of living there, the experience of such a house must be what life's all about.

Then you open the door, you walk in and your eyes meet the reality of your expectations. You engage the entrance and find your expectations hitting the floor in an overwhelming amount of items. It feels like this particular family has been moving many times, lived in many different homes, with many different styles, but they haven't thrown anything out over the years. They keep on hoarding, accumulating new functionality, new designs, new directions. They don't throw anything out.

In the kitchen, three refrigerators competes for a purpose. One is starting to make strange and loud sounds after thirty years. The second was bought unknowing that the third would be released the year after as a state-of-the-art in design and functionality, a bit over engineered. In the living room, surrounding a huge dining table, capable of seating twelve people, three out of twelve chairs are in a different unique style with no common art direction, failing to bring synergy to the room. The bedroom offers two choices of scales, one digital and another analogue, both equally god, though you enjoy the look of the analogue and the functionality of the digital.

You could make the argument, it is what it is, that this family know and understand the situation, gradually adding, without removing, replacing or changing. Comfortably enjoying the new and reminiscing about the old. Surrounded with great memories and accomplishments, quietly fading into the background and out of attention. But is that serene living, is that freedom and relaxation?

The problem is the concept space, the ruling frame that each concept lives within. Each concept has such a space, a set of restrictions that will apply to its definition, giving the product nuance, ingenuity, beauty, essence, a true and thoughtful user experience. When you can't remove items from your concept space, you can't limit the space and it will keep growing, clouding, overwhelming and burden the user in its path. Each new concept entering the space will suffer under this weight, this cloud of legacy and culture, failing to add pure untainted value, but instead adding more weight.

There are no rules, no principals applied to the household for maintaining the space and in the end, the space will collapse under its own weight.

When we can apply principles to the concept, removing features that either contradict or are no longer of purpose, we can create synergetic experiences within the household, as all elements must work together.

A principle rule must be based on the initial learnings of a challenge and the executed validation of an achievement. While the challenge will explore the feasibility of a principle, the achievement will validate the foundation and truth of the principle. As most principles are based on goals and wishes, they rarely holds any merits and practical sustainability. I have been in countless meetings with the phrase, "write that down as a principle", uttered in the hope to implement a theoretical rule, forcing an unsubstantial principle into the product, skipping the logic where it feels convenient. Instead of saying, "write that down as a challenge or as an achievement", we now have to struggle with a theoretical rule that might not hold any merit towards the customer-centric design, thus falling into the category of ego-centric design.

Principle rules must be implemented because they make sense and has passed the test of time and purpose. They will make sure we keep our focus and follow a minimum standard, aligning our efforts and product viability.

As an example, a principle rule that states, "all headlines must be in capital letters", has to be able to answer the challenge of why, and the achievement of how. If I can't answer why all headlines should be in capital letters, then I fail the first test towards creating my principle rule. Secondly, if I can't tell how to create all headlines in capital letters, then I fail the second test.

CREATE A PRINCIPLE BY PROOFING IT AGAINST *WHY* AND *HOW*

People involved in the design process can be defined by three degrees of perspective, the executive as the business strategic, the director as the concept theoretic and the developer as the design practitioner. This structure can be a simile to how some of the most accomplished builders gain progress and results, the bee hive.

Within the hive, the queen instructs the soldiers, who manage the workers, who performs the practice. Each communicating on different levels and with a different perspective and understanding. To understand the language, you must understand how each degree of perspective will relate to the language.

The queen is interested in accents, which is the principles for scoping her soldiers. With an accent you define a direction and with multiple accents, you can define multiple directions.

The soldiers are interested in structure, which is the process for instructing their workers. Each structure is created in relation to the accent and when the accent evolve, so will the structure, as it must adjust to the changes or collapse.

The workers are interested the dictionary, which is the best practice approach, for archiving the principles. The dictionary is build on the soldiers structure and each learning is added to the dictionary, as it contains the company design knowledge as principles.

A principle rule must be based on the initial learnings of a challenge and the executed validation of an achievement. While the challenge will explore the feasibility of a principle, the achievement will validate the foundation and truth of the principle. As most principles are based on goals and wishes, they rarely holds any merits and practical sustainability. I have been in countless meetings with the phrase, "write that down as a principle", uttered in the hope to implement a theoretical rule, forcing an unsubstantial principle into the product, skipping the logic where it feels convenient. Instead of saying, "write that down as a challenge or as an achievement", we now have to struggle with a theoretical rule that might not hold any merit towards the user-centric design, thus falling into the category of ego-centric design.

Principle rules must be implemented because they make sense and has passed the test of time and purpose. They will make sure we keep our focus and follow a minimum standard, aligning our efforts and product viability.

As an example, a principle rule that states, "all headlines must be in capital letters", has to be able to answer the challenge of why, and the achievement of how. If I can't answer why all headlines should be in capital letters, then I fail the first test towards creating my principle rule. Secondly, if I can't tell how to create all headlines in capital letters, then I fail the second test.

Create a principle by proofing it against why and how.

A QUEENS ACCENT

When creating a product line, each design has a purpose and thus a persona, a receiver. The persona has an accent, a preferred understanding within the language, a way to communicate back and forth, the purpose, between design and persona.

Design is not tailored to one person, its created for a group, and it's the generalization of this group that becomes your target audience. Merging your audience into one person, creates a simplified face for your design and a benchmark for your progress. The size of your audience will be in proportions to the amount of work you need to put into your design.

Working with a large audience group, will create more attention to your details and your process. There will be many different user reactions that your design should be able to absorb. A large group will be more demanding, less tolerant and more critical, putting stress on your design. It's in such a group that your true skills as a designer will be highly visible.

When you merge a large group, your design will have to speak to allot of different people making your entire process more complex, creating exes attention to every step. You need to further polish and evaluate your strategies, studies and research, taking every aspect of your group into account.

Just like an engine, communicating through your design is about action and reaction. The more fuel you put into your engine, the more reaction you get and vice versa - the more reaction you want, the more fuel you'll need. Using this analogy, you can measure the amount of work you need to put into your designs, with the amount of users you want to captivate with each piece of your product. The ability to put all the pieces together in the right order, will create a stunning image of communication.

Your target group is synthesized into one personality, the persona, as your exploration dictates, who becomes the tone of your accent. Your persona is the reincarnation and embodiment of market feedback and opportunities, which you must achieve as a designer.

Traditional persona theory states that you define an archetype, a static face, but a modern strategy must move with the extreme forces of quickly shifting markets and trends. As the market shifts, so will the persona, as it's grounded in the insight of your business studies. Creating a persona, a relatable personality, will also serve to ignite the emotional synergy between designer, product and user. The designer will bond with the persona and the persona must be bonded with product.

Your principles will be the validator and business goals, the metric you judge your thoughts against. By aligning your ideas, following simple phrases, you will stay true to your purpose, the goal and then create a strong coherent product line.

A designer must have a set of accents applied with both personas and principals. Each accent is based on the premise of a goal, the principal, and a target, the persona experiencing the goal.

The accent will be a container of the static and reliable principles, tested over time by the dynamic and unpredictable persona. This creates two poles of detraction, a magnetic balanced design language, hold together by the customers attraction. When you apply an accent to your designs, you apply a guideline, a set rules that will hold you on the right track. The accent will become your measurement, your validation and acceptance.

A SOLDIERS GRAMMAR

The language structure defines the grammar of your language elements and the process for archiving results, implementing routines and methods. A design language is constructed by signs, connected by a code to their meaning.

By creating a language on signs, code and meaning, you create a grammar for you designs that will be more flexible and adaptable than any static design guide. When words are expressed and related to other words, they form sentences and understanding. In a design language, a word is a sign, the expression is the code that pronounce the sign and the relation binds the sign to a sentence, creating meaning. Defining the three aspects of your language, will define your accent as a principle and scientific design guide.

1. **Signs**, is the words in your language, defined by buttons, knobs, gestures, light, sound, display, iconography, typography and symbolisms in your language accent. Each, is a way to communicate with the user, as the user will relate to the product through these elements of interaction. By understanding and defining the purpose of each sign, you can build your accent as a coherent instrument, recreating a fine-tuned communication from product to product, and area to area.
2. **Code**, is the expressions and mannerisms in your language, defined by opacity, color, weight, texture and style. Each code will add or subtract the subtlety, as the code will slightly alter the pronunciation of a sign.
3. **Meaning**, is the relationship in your language, the science between padding and margin. Calculating the distance between signs, defines the relationship between parent, child and sibling signs, establishing the ability to understand your language through structure and relation. When you add signs together in this structure, you start to form intuitive sentences.

Knowing the family, the story each sign tells and the heritage of the family tree, will help you understand your interactions. As you define your accent by defining meanings, codes and signs, you will gain a language grammar for coherent product designs, in each accent you use.

Even though your design language is a creation of yours, it will still be based on the heritage of other design languages. English, a language that is derived from latin, is constantly incorporating signs, codes and meanings from other languages, such as french and dutch. This is a natural evolution, where speech is evolving between borders. Like a spoken language, your design language will also evolve and each sign, code and meaning will be compared to the world of languages, from which the initial learning will start for your customers.

When a customer starts to learn your language, they borrow the meaning from the languages they already know. If you incorporate signs, codes and meaning, closely related to what they know, but slightly altered in either sign, code or meaning, the learning curve will be low. When you introduce new and unknown elements to any language, you must use your design language structure to give them a learning path.

A designers language will define a balance between the principle theory that must be challenged and the dynamic quickly shifting persona theory, that must be restrained. Adding the two theories to a language as a guide, specialized through an accent, will create an evolving design process, replacing the deprecated and static design manuals in a modern world.

A WORKERS DICTIONARY

A common mistake in design strategies and manuals, is the consistency across all efforts, as this is meant to keep a tone of voice over time. All design areas must be adaptable to the situation, time, location and media, so must the design language, implemented as a coherent tone-of-voice instead of a consistent. Coherent design is about keeping the essence, within an adaptable language, thus must the language be about the interpretation, defining the constructs of why, not how, to communicate your product.

Many companies spend months, years and decades refining, updating and reimplementing their design manuals in a hopeless race against *why* and *how*. The manual serve as a reminder for the principles and goals the company had, at the time the strategy was created. But at the time the manual is done, the company principles and goals are now different, thus fighting to be consistent and relevant in a market on the move.

When you know how to speak a language, you can only replicate it, just like children do with their native language, i.e. "monkey see, monkey do". This is how design manuals work, as design elements like headlines, columns, fonts and colors are carefully defining how to replicate them in minute details. Each element of design is shown as a recipe. The problem arise when your recipe doesn't account for the new or different situations, that your design must adapt to. Like a headline defining the specific size and margins in pixels, which might not translate to other medias, packaging, cultures or countries.

When you know why you speak a language, you can teach it, express it and adapt it, without loosing its meaning. If you understand why a headline should have a certain size and margin, without defining the specifics, you can adapt those principles to your current situation, without breaking the design language.

The design dictionary is a modern day design guide with a more agile and dynamic implementation, as we set the rules of our language elements and create examples for best practice as principles, creating routines and setting standards. But these rules are not defined in specifics, they are the results of the language structure that controls each element.

A design manual is a consistent design strategy, where a design language is a coherent design strategy, based on an accent, a structure and a dictionary.

SECTION 4

SOLUTION

Solution, a united and focused direction from current goals. Design must be finite and uncompromised. Pick your battles, double down and spend time together.

Don't waste your time in the final stages of the production, fine-tuning over wireframes, writing adjustments briefs or managing complex specification sheets. These are all valid in the application phase, to define an overview, but no amount of documentation or illustration will ever substitute the need for eye-to-eye workshops, as the solution is finalizing.

As you reach the final sprint, the details become blurry and increasingly forgettable, as the goal is within reach, racing towards the finish line. The shortest destination between two minds, is face to face. Don't waste your time transcending your perception and thoughts into briefs, when the most prudent outcome and culturing evolvement, is in person, overseeing the minute details, which can often be neglected or down prioritized.

If you often fight executive management on a products viability, then your organization isn't build for the disruptive potential of your product. The ability the drive new opportunities through the established processes, creating disruptive products for market vacuums, most be driven through a disruptive capable processes, in contrast and opposite to the sustaining process.

The strength of your organization is your core believe, the why, how and what. This is your core expertise as an organization and should reside as an internal force. Everything that falls outside your core expertise or your core predicted expertise in the future, should and must be outsourced to those where this is their core expertise. This doesn't mean that an entire methodology should be outsourced, but the element of that process, which is not within your core expertise. Companies can be divided into three categories, on the question of outsourcing, as a brand-only, creative or production company.

1. **Brand-only**, those who only focus on their name, their brand and the service surrounding the outsourced expertise. These companies often excels in the ability to brand their name and services, as this is their core expertise, focusing on the experience in their product design, outsourcing the story, function and journey.
2. **Creative**, those who outsource production, as they focus on retaining the creative credibility behind their name, their brand and the surrounding services. These companies are often more interested in the product story, journey and experience, retaining their creative ability as they define them self as design managers, which often conflict with the outsourcing of functionality.

3. **Production**, those who retain a specific in-house production, which is acquired for brand and creative companies. These companies are often function attentive and are wining fast market shares, based on their ability to provide valid and polished functionality to those who outsource this ability. As they are focusing on functionality, they might not excel in creating a name for them self, as they serve from behind the scenes. Some companies in these situations are creating new companies, providing functionality to their spinoffs, who compete on the same level as their own clients.

Working with the design agency TBWA, also known as Apple's agency through many years, their organizational expertise is to tell creative and conceptual stories for their clients, bringing client brand, customers and experiences together as a creative company, with magical results. Their expertise is not in the functional production of their stories, as this is a fast paced technical area in a digital age, where new technologies raise and fall on a daily basis.

In order to secure the same level of details in their practical work, as they had put into their theoretical work, I implemented a methodology from a series of stages, where each stage would define the input and output from either internal or external resources. This methodology gave TBWA the ability to pick and choose from the variety of cases they obtained from their clients, using the best combination of internal or external resources on a case by case basis. This approach also gave them the ability to experiments with more or less outsourcing, to test the validity in both internal and external work.

Outsourcing is not a relationship, outsourcing is a factory. You need to define the details in all the areas that matters, business and brand, before you involve your factory. Every detail specified and prototyped, will become subject to interpretation. They don't perceive your culture, view, understanding and legacy, why would they understand the details in a process where you might struggle to define them for yourself.

Outsourcing digital or conceptual ideas, must be similar to outsourcing the production of physical objects, make it about pure production, not creativity, as you should either retain or obtain such skills. This process must be overseen by a key creative lead at both ends, merging the culture and the perspective. You wouldn't outsource your identity, your unique approach, but instead, inspire, teach, learn and share with their creative lead.

The most common outcome of outsourcing, is the tendency to reinvent the entire product strategy. As the outsourcing agency is viewing your product as fresh piece of paper, everything becomes possible and they fall into the trap of reinventing the status quo. Through extensive work, they reach what you already know, that there are limitations and possibilities in every corner. As they are unaware of these corners, they start to explore the canvas, reaching conclusions that was redundant. This approach can be an inspiration, if that is the intension, to seek new opportunities in the early stages on concept development. But as you reach the final stages, outsourcing has to be kept to pure production, while they must understand why and how the concept came to be, without trying to change to results by their implied limited knowledge of the concept. Their focus must be on the how, while you must make them understand the why, as you retain the principle role.

THE DEVIL IS IN THE DETAILS

While reaching the final design stages, the product is starting to look and present as intended. It is in this final stage that you must be extra attentive to the details as you can quickly lose focus on the project at hand, shifting your attention to the next project.

There is a level of understanding that any designer gain through decades of experiences. This knowledge has been build from a focused and attentive interest in design and through this attention, we can see the hidden details, the missing or misplaced elements. When polishing the wrinkles, a common respond from my colleagues has always been, “I don’t see it, it looks fine to me!”. This is often the respond of people who are attentive on other areas than design, building their knowledge from a different focus, like engineers and project managers.

When I listen to classical music, I can't understand the nodes and to me, it sounds like noise. The same happens to any of us, when we listen to a language that is different from what we know and care about. When we speak a native language, thought by woven knowledge, we don't think about why we do it, we just know how to do it. As all areas of knowledge is a language, so is design a language, one we must define and express. This language is not intended to be taught, but to be experienced. We all have an area of expertise, an area that we understands the subtleties of, the hidden nodes that others can't hear, because they don't understand the details.

In design, these details are often neglected as unnoticeable, simply because they are managed by people who can't see the errors in their actions, unable to see the details or the lack thereof. As a design manager, you must be able to see the details, as you must be able to understand the language that you are communicating. If you don't understand the language, you can't communicate with your target segment, thus failing to move your customers with a designed experience, which then fails to resonate, furthermore, fails to gain loyalty. Loyalty is an automatic guaranteed repeat business and word of mouth recognition, a measurable investment.

Simply because you can't see, hear or taste it, doesn't mean it isn't there. When it is there, you can feel the difference, as we are experiencing a beautiful journey of functional stories. When you care for the details, your customers will experience the subtleties, establishing an unconscious emotional bond with the product, achieving the luxurious moment.

EXPONENTIAL DESIGN WEIGHT

When designers are defining poetic stories, they need to be able to break it into a methodology for creating the foundation, supporting their vision. When their vision is passing through story, function, journey and experience, the vision is gaining weight through each of these achievements. This weight is an analogy for the increasing advanced attention and knowledge, that the product design requires. As the story, the product heart, is evolving into the basic skeleton and the journey is adding muscles, this structure must be able to hold and support the final layer of skin, when the experience is added. The algorithm in this process, should assume that each achievement will double in weight, thus requiring more knowledge and attention by each achievement. As there are four basic achievements, the story will multiply eight times in weight, as the methodology of design is finalizing the product. Most products fail to hit its deadline and resource allocation, simply because there hasn't been allocated enough knowledge and attention by each achievement, and that each achievement is not accounting for the increasing weight added by the next. This often leads to products over due or collapsing under its own weight. The final achievement alone, the experience, will be responsible for 50% of the total weight throughout the project.

The exponential design weight algorithm (EDW) is also the basis for the structured achievement order of story, function, journey and experience, as each achievement is both supporting and accounting for the next. By going through this specific order, the product will be able to support and deliver as a project, by designing the product from the core, following the user through each achievement, increasingly adding knowledge and attention. Each layer added, can be calculated and tailored as the product is gaining structure and validation from the inside out.

The work of the design team, the time spend on research, applying knowledge and prototyping; is defined as design weight, summarized as an index number. This number will define the amount of weight on each achievement, as the next will double that number. Imagine the weight of an elephant, growing from an infant story into a mature and adult elephant experience.

As each achievement continuously double the index, the last achievement will be the heaviest and the achievement where most amount of senior knowledge, attention and resources should be allocated. This is often not the case, when the final achievement is rushed through product creation, crippling the product, as the weight isn't capable of supporting the vision in the end. When this happens, reinforcements are added to the structure to make it stand, destroying the poetic beauty when compromises must be made. The outer experience layer is falling apart, as the structure must be re-molded, unable to withhold the experience, which was created for a different structure. The story at the core of the product, is now unable to express its vision, as the experience layer is destroyed, the layer responsible for communicating and resonating with the customer.

Creating the story, the idea, is an easy design weight to lift, as the complexity is on a theoretical level. But when you reach the experience, after going through function and journey, the weight will be eight times heavier, meaning that the required knowledge and attention, in contrast to the story, will be eight times more demanding and critical. When the product is reaching the final achievement, the experience has to bond with the user in an emotional relation. This achievement is not an easy task, as the complexity and required design skills are exponentially high, when story has to be expressed in artistry, through journey and function. If the journey and function achievements hasn't accounted for the complex experience achievement, the project will fall apart.

In short, if it required above average intelligence to deliver the story, it will require exceptionally gifted intelligence to deliver the final product. As the story becomes more complex, so will the required and exponential knowledge, to achieve the product.

In many companies, creative thinking is perceived as the highest intelligence in the company, where functionality is just a task to be done. This misdirected perception and the neglecting of design weight, is what hinders product design in achieving its maximum potential, as the vision can't be created and expressed by people unable to understand the visionary.

Through challenges and achievements, perception and management, allocating the required knowledge will make the product plausible. But it's important to accept the advanced and demanding process of achieving design and that each achievement will only get more demanding. That the gifted idea, might not be possible because of the exponential requirements.

SUMMARY

Through this book I have told you of the risky challenges and changeable achievements of design, describing the single mind and the collective team through management, as design has to be balanced from all angles. The most important learnings from this book is in the term creative balance, to be open and honest with yourself, to understand your organization and channel your focus, setting an example by your actions and results.

You know design is not a matter of taste, that design is not just a style nor a simple step by step process, as it's an ideology and a believe to balance and understand the customer through creativity, insights, empathy and science.

You often see either the *why* or the *how* in an agency, depending on their culture, creating an almost religious believe in either defending challenges or achievements. Though most people don't implement design in those terms, the synergy of using both challenges and achievements to balance design, is common.

In the software industry, hackers are often invited to participate in the test and validation of the safety and security of operating systems or personal data platforms. They are, in this context, the challengers to the developers achievements. As the development has been focusing on the *how*, the hackers will reverse engineer, challenging the *how* into the *why*. The same is seen in banking and financial sectors, where hackers are testing the plausibility of entering the achievement of what should be impossible to penetrate. This is becoming a standard in software, where the why is added as a precaution, instead of implementing it as part of the development, it becomes a nice-to-have.

In the food industry, the journalistic critics, challenge the restaurants and their gourmet achievements. As each aspiring chef is adding every layer of creativity into his or her dining experience, the focus is on achieving, the how, neglecting to understand the challenge, the why. To create the perfect dish, the why must be their initial thought, thus knowing how to meet the critics.

As the why is often seen trailing the how, many products suffer from reverse engineering, as the achievements are meeting the challenges as an end result. To succeed in achieving, you must understand your challenge before embarking on your path to victory.

This simple dilemma is found within all areas of business, even is efficient design driven organizations, where products or visions are presented to the board of directors as how, hoping to get funding or budget approvals. The approach should be reversed, e.g. what is the budget or economical perspective, then finding the answers to achieving that challenge.

It is important to constantly evolve on your designs, your process and your skills. Without these basic principles, your designs will become unbalanced and drift away from core believes and your costumer target base, no matter how loyal a base you have obtained. Even highly balanced designs that yields an almost fanatic and loving customer base, will eventually die with the customers, if the design isn't evolving with new customer age segments. Unbalanced design will face the tiering and tedious task of constantly working for the costumers loyalty, as they yield very little emotional relationship with the customers. An unbalanced design is quickly seen as odd or dysfunctional, as there is something off, something that doesn't seems to be thoroughly designed, that little frown in the face of your customer, when they feel compromised in their purchase, resulting in buyers remorse.

TRANSFORMING AN ORGANIZATION

To break the rules in an organization, your must first understand and accept them, in order to redefine them. Change is a great thing, as we get the excitement of the unknown and the knowledge of going through the learnings, understanding new possibilities. The change might not be a success, never the less, the change will uncover new insight that will forever be part of the culture and future challenges.

Creating true changes, is a transformation. Changes can be reversed, where as a transformation is irreversible. When you transform, you become something new, something that you haven't been before, an emerging evolution, forcing your thoughts, emotions and practices into a new direction.

A transformation will be more than a journey of learnings, ups and downs, it will require that you let go, breaking the bond with safety and dive in to the deep waters. As the waves washes over your decisions, you need a railing to hold on to, a methodology to guide you through the storm and stay faithful to your path.

Design as a business, is not a change, but a transformation, a revolution in creating superior products, a believe in design as an ideology. This revolution has been simmering for decades, beginning in the early 2000 when information architecture (IA) become the new trend, putting pressure on the common art director. We needed more than an eye for colors and typography. Soon, user interaction designers (UI) would emerge, followed by user experience designers (UX) in 2005. UX started to evolve as a holistic business approach, emerging as service design and customer experience (CX) design, a way to mange and drive customer-centric services and processes.

Promising titles, job descriptions and personalities within these emerging areas, could hold the key to this transformation. But working in larger organizations, located at the bottom of the design latter, will require more than great skills and good intensions. It will require that you balance business, change and risk management, to set the wheels in motion, creating small droplets in the water, progressing, building towards the wave, the true change, the irreversible transformation.

To pursue a design ideology, you must believe in your path and in your choices. You must stand as an example, becoming an inspiration by the work you do. We can all trust the act of changes, well knowing that it won't last, but to transform, you must believe that you'll succeed. Do not try to teach or instruct your intensions, instead, show them your intensions, by proving your believe in the work you do. Let your results, the success of your challenges and achievements, stand as a statement for the transformation you seek to implement.

For people to believe in progressive experience (PX) design, it is important to show them how. For people to trust progressive design, it is important to show them why.

If people believe, they will follow.

If people trust, they will lead.

Design must be in harmonic balance, as you must incorporate multiple angles to understand, learn and achieve. If we only focus on the narrow perspective, we loose focus on the goal and the broad view of things. We must be able to see the horizon, as we must know the problems from all angles. Creativity is not just an artistic expression, as creativity is part of all thoughts, actions and methods.

The secret to success, is knowledge!

PROGRESSIVE DESIGN SOLUTION

The second book in the Progressive Design series, explores the methodology in details...

In the book *Progressive Design Solution*, I'll define the sixteen stages of progressive experience (PX) design, diving into the details, the practicality and template for creating design as a business, within an organization. From each stage, you'll understand the process and the work that will evolve your design and move your project forward, step by step.

Each stage approaches design as it was meant to be, a tangible ideology; enlightening business models, employee knowledge and customer believe. It implements multiple processes, combining them into the four principles of design, covering all angles as a methodology, a template. This template can be applied to any company structure, from startups to fortune 500 enterprises, from lean and agile movements to static and rigorous processes.

AFTERWORDS

Perceive. Challenge. Achieve. Manage.

My work in this book is ongoing and I hope you have enjoyed this current edition. If you wish to follow, contact, comment or inspire the next edition, then connect with me on the social networks. For additional books, articles and cases, go to my website at lindborg.io.

MOVEMENT

Join the progressive design

movement at dsgnr.io

CPSIA information can be obtained at www.ICGtesting.com
Printed in the USA
LVOW08s2018180215

427448LV00018B/932/P

9 781503 296145